THE PANTON BOOK
OF PUNGENT
PROVERBS

Dépôt légal/2ème trimestre 1986
Bibliothèque Nationale du Canada
Bibliothèque Nationale du Québec

Printed in Canada by Marcel Didier inc. with permission of the Copyright's
owner for exclusive distribution in Canada, the United States of America
and their territories.

Distribution: Hurtubise HMH - Didier
              7360 Bd Newman
              Ville de LaSalle (Québec)
              Canada   H8N 1X2
              Telex: 055-6767 MARDIDCAN
              Telephone: (514) 364-0323

First published 1982
ISBN 2-89144-121-4

PROVERBS

Proverbes

Sprichwörter

Proverbios

Proverbi

INTRODUCTION

Human experience of one kind or another lies at the origin of most proverbs. It is, we are told, "the mother of wisdom", the potted wisdom of Man since first he became articulate. There is an old Russian proverb which says: "The horses of hope gallop, but the asses of wisdom go slowly". Not, of course, when they have a pack of wolves at their heels, unless we are to believe that "more haste, less speed" is invariably true, which it isn't, since "those who hesitate are lost", even asses. Reverse that advice and what are we told? "Look before you leap", a warning uttered in solemn tones by prudent fathers to unheeding youngsters. Strange how proverbs contradict one another, but that is the way of life. We live in a world of contradictions, and it is in finding our way through the cross-currents that we learn that men are "as different as chalk from cheese" in spite of the Italian reminder that "people are the same the whole world over".

One thing I have noticed about proverbs is that they frequently spring from familiar situations of the kind that lend themselves to graphic representation. Silvia Mondini has made good use of this in her drawings, many of which are full of the humour and satire beloved by caricaturists. Abstract sayings like "knowledge is power" and "prevention is better than cure" are ponderous and best left alone. To depict Pope's famous line "the proper study of mankind is man" would be tedious and the result anything but pungent. Yet in those seven words Pope recommended a subject that gains much in depth and interest from a study of proverbs.

This book of "Pungent Proverbs" is not for study purposes. It is meant to entertain, to introduce the reader to the vast store of popular sayings contained in The Oxford Dictionary of English Proverbs *by William Smith (O.U.P.), in* English Proverbs Explained *by Ronald Ridout and Clifford Witting (Pan Books), and by Patricia Houghton in her* World of Proverbs *(Blandford Press). There one can delve into the rich loam of common sense which has helped to bring Man back to the path of reason and sanity ever since he began to reflect on the nature of the world and his existence.*

The Bible contains many heartening reminders that proverbs were in common use even before the time of Christ. "The spirit is willing, but the flesh is weak," Christ said to Peter in the Garden of Gethsemane. "Spare the rod and spoil the child," comes, most appropriately, from the Book of Proverbs. *For the assurance that "no man can serve two masters" and that "the labourer is worthy of his hire" we must, however, turn to the* New Testament: *to* St Matthew *for "by their fruits ye shall know them". Some of these sacred chestnuts could well be illustrated. Not all, though, for they belong to a tradition that demands reverence. They are rubies on the thread of life and, as such, they deserve respect.*

It is the more homely type of proverb and saying that our artist has sought in her own way to interpret, the type that falls from the lips according to the circumstances of the moment. "Charity begins at home" is one, "as you make your bed, so you must lie on it" is another; or, again, "don't wash your dirty linen in public". They give force to our reactions to commonplace situations, pleasant and unpleasant. If, in our youth, we had heeded such words of elementary wisdom as "you cannot have your cake and eat it", or "you cannot burn the candle at both ends", our lives might have turned out very differently. But then, as people say, "you cannot put old heads on young shoulders".

There must, I am sure, be a proverb "to fit the bill" on almost every occasion. It may not always spring to mind, but that is itself a challenge to look for one: "nothing seek, nothing find" can be said with equal truth when looking for a proverb as when drilling for oil in the back garden. In Italian "chi cerca trova", which goes to show that people think alike, though they express themselves in varying degrees of emphasis in English, French, German, Spanish and Italian. That is perfectly understandable. What is less so is that although we are more closely knit than ever before, proverbs of modern idiom do not seem to find their way into these languages.

The trouble is that we no longer make them up, perhaps because life is too hectic to leave time for creating new aphorisms. Instead, we fall back on sayings like "it's useless to flog a dead horse" when the car won't start and we feel like kicking it. Cars, TV sets, videotapes, computers have not been with us long enough to win a place in the language of proverbs. There are plenty of slogans about consumer products, but no proverbs! They would not have the bouquet that goes with a mature adage, so we rely on the old ones. As our illustrations prove, it takes an artist to lift them from the past and put them into a modern setting.

Michael Langley

1 Tous ceux qui vont à l'église ne sont pas des saints.

No todos los que estudian son letrados.

Nicht nur Heilige gehen zur Kirche.

Non son tutti santi quelli che vanno in chiesa.

2 Tout est bien qui finit bien.

Bien está lo que bien acaba.

Ende gut, alles gut.

Tutto è bene quel che finisce bene.

3 Tel travail, tel salaire.

A tal trabajo, tal salario.

Wie die Arbeit, so der Lohn.

Tale il lavoro, tale il salario.

4 Comme on fait son lit, on se couche.

Quien mala cama hace, en ella yace.

Wie man sich bettet, so liegt man.

Come uno si fa il letto, così dorme.

5 Demande beaucoup pour avoir un peu.

Pide lo más, y algo te darán,

Wer etwas will, muß vieles fordern.

Chi vuole assai, non domandi poco.

6 La beauté est éphémère.

Hermosura, al fin basura.

Auf die inneren Werte kommt es an.

La bellezza è effimera.

7 Mieux vaut être seul qu'en mauvaise compagnie.

Mejor solo que mal acompañado.

Besser allein als in schlechter Gesellschaft.

Meglio soli che male accompagnati.

8 Mieux vaut un oeuf aujourd'hui qu'une poule demain.

Mejor es huevo hoy que pollo mañana.

Lieber den Spatz in der Hand als die Taube auf dem Dach.

Meglio un uovo oggi che una gallina domani.

9 Faute de grives, on mange des merles.

A falta de pan, buenas son tortas.

Besser ein kleiner Fisch als gar nichts auf dem Tisch.

Meglio poco che niente.

10 Mieux vaut aller au paradis en haillons qu'en enfer en habit de dentelle.

Besser arm in Ehren als reich in Schanden.

Más vale honra sin barcos que barcos sin honra.

Meglio povertà onorata che ricchezza svergognata.

11 Mieux vaut tard que jamais.   Lieber spät als nie.

Más vale tarde que nunca.   Meglio tardi che mai.

12 Qui se ressemble s'assemble.

Cada oveja con su pareja.

Gleich und gleich gesellt sich gern.

I simili vanno con i simili.

13 Les affaires sont les affaires.

El negocio es el negocio.

Geschäft ist Geschäft.

Gli affari sono affari.

14 Qui ne fait rien fait mal.

Müßiggang ist aller Laster Anfang.

Muchos males engendra la ociosidad.

L'ozio è il padre dei vizi.

15 Nul avant sa mort ne peut être dit heureux.

Nadie se alabe hasta que acabe.

Keiner ist vor seinem Tod glücklich zu preisen.

Nessuno può dirsi felice a questo mondo.

16 Les soucis font blanchir
les cheveux de bonne heure.

Quien se apura, su muerte
apresura.

Übertriebene Fürsorge
schadet nur.

Le preoccupazioni fanno
venire i capelli bianchi.

17 Un chien regarde bien un évêque.

El perro puede mirar al rey.

Auch ein König ist nur ein Mensch.

Anche un gatto può guardare un re.

18 Charité bien ordonnée
commence par soi-même.

Wohltun beginnt zu Hause.

La caridad bien entendida
empieza por uno mismo.

La prima carità comincia
da se stessi.

19 Ce que l'enfant entend au foyer est bientôt connu jusqu'au moustier.

Lo que el niño oyó en el hogar, eso dice en el portal.

Wie die Alten sungen, so zwitschern auch die Jungen.

I bambini ripetono ciò che hanno sentito in casa.

20 A main froide, coeur chaud.   Kalte Hände, warmes Herz.

Manos frías, corazón caliente.   Mani fredde, cuore caldo.

21 Comparaison n'est pas raison.   Jeder Vergleich hinkt.

Toda comparación es odiosa.   I confronti sono odiosi.

22 Chacun loue son oeuvre.

Cada ollero su olla alaba.

Jeder Krämer lobt seine Ware.

Ognuno loda il suo operato.

23 Il a les yeux plus grands que le ventre.

Se llena antes el papo que el ojo.

Die Augen sind oft größer als der Magen.

Ha gli occhi più grandi della bocca.

24 La familiarité engendre
le mépris.

Vertraulichkeit schadet
dem Respekt.

La familiaridad es causa
de menosprecio.

Troppa confidenza toglie
riverenza.

25 Le feu et l'eau sont bons serviteurs mais mauvais maîtres.

Feuer und Wasser sind zwei gute Diener, aber zwei schlimme Herren.

El fuego y el agua son buenos servidores pero ruines amos.

Il fuoco e l'acqua son buoni servitori, ma cattivi padroni.

26 Premier arrivé, premier servi.

El primer venido, primer servido.

Wer zuerst kommt, mahlt zuerst.

Chi tardi arriva, male alloggia.

27 Le fou et son argent sont bientôt séparés.

El tonto y su dinero son pronto separados.

Ein Narr und sein Geld sind nicht lange Freund in der Welt.

Il pazzo e il suo denaro son presto separati.

28 Quatre yeux voient mieux que deux.

Cuatro ojos ven más que dos.

Vier Augen sehen mehr als zwei.

Quattro occhi vedono più di due.

29 L'habit fait l'homme.

El hábito hace al monje.

Kleider machen Leute.

L'abito fa l'uomo.

30 Dieu fit la campagne, l'homme fit la ville.

Dios hizo el campo y el hombre la ciudad.

Gott schuf die Natur, die Städte sind vom Menschen.

Dio fece la campagna, l'uomo fece la città.

31 Bon cheval n'a pas besoin d'éperon.

Caballo que vuela, no quiere espuelas.

Ein williges Pferd soll man nicht spornen.

Caval che corre non ha bisogno di sprone.

32 Diversité réjouit.

En la variedad está el gusto.

In der Abwechslung liegt das Vergnügen.

Il piacere sta nella varietà.

33 L'habitude est une seconde nature.

La costumbre es otra naturaleza.

Gewohnheiten gehen in Fleisch und Blut über.

L'abitudine è una seconda natura.

34 Trop presser nuit.

Cosa hecha aprisa, cosa
de risa.

Blinder Eifer schadet nur.

Troppa fretta nuoce.

35 Santé passe richesse.

Gesundheit ist das höchste Gut.

Primero es la salud que el dinero.

La salute val più della ricchezza.

36 Il cuit dans son jus.

Er soll in seinem eigenen
Saft schmoren.

Se cuece en su propia salsa.

Bisogna lasciarlo cuocere
nel suo brodo.

37 Il est armé de pied en cap.

Está armado hasta los dientes.

Er ist bis an die Zähne bewaffnet.

È armato fino ai denti.

38 Il a un pied dans la tombe.

Er steht mit einem Fuß im Grab.

Está con un pie en la sepultura.

Ha un piede nella fossa.

39 Il me mène par le bout du nez.

Er führt mich an der Nase herum.

Me tiene agarrado por las narices.

Mi sta menando per il naso.

40 Il est sur des épines.

Está sobre espinas.

Er sitzt wie auf Nadeln.

Sta sulle spine.

41 Il m'a mis la puce à l'oreille.

Me ha echado la pulga detrás de la oreja.

Er hat mir einen Floh ins Ohr gesetzt.

Mi ha messo una pulce nell'orecchio.

42 Il a filé à l'anglaise.

Er hat sich französisch empfohlen.

Se despide a la francesa.

Se n'è andato all'inglese.

43 Qui achète ce dont il n'a pas besoin devra vendre ce qu'il ne voudrait pas.

Qien compra lo que no puede, vende lo que le duele.

Wer Unnötiges kauft, muß bald Notwendiges verkaufen.

Chi compra il superfluo, venderà il necessario.

44 Qui se couche avec des chiens se lève avec des puces.

Legst Du Dich mit den Hunden, so stehst Du mit den Flöhen auf.

Quien con perros se acuesta, con pulgas se levanta.

Chi va a letto con i cani, si leva con le pulci.

45 En épousant sa femme pour son argent, il a vendu sa liberté.

En casa de mujer rica, ella manda y ella grita.

Für Geld gefreit, ein goldnes Joch.

Dove entra dote, esce libertà.

46 Qui s'excuse, s'accuse.

Quien se excusa, se acusa.

Wer sich entschuldigt, klagt sich an.

Chi si scusa, si accusa.

47 Qui cherche, trouve.

Quien busca, halla.

Wer sucht, der findet.

Chi cerca, trova.

48 On s'instruit en voyageant.   Reisen bildet.

Viajando se instruye la gente.   Chi viaggia, si istruisce.

49 L'honnêteté est le meilleur des guides.

Ehrlich währt am längsten.

La honradez es el mejor capital.

L'onestà è la miglior moneta.

50 La maison fait connaître
le maître.

Man sieht am Hause, wes
Sinnes der Herr ist.

Por la casa se conoce al dueño.

Dalla casa si conosce
il padrone.

51 Il n'est sauce que d'appétit.

Hunger ist der beste Koch.

A buen hambre no hay pan duro.

La fame è il miglior cuoco.

52 Si tu veux la paix,
prépare la guerre.

Si quieres la paz, prepárate
para la guerra.

Wer Frieden haben will, muß
zum Krieg rüsten.

Chi vuol la pace, apparecchi
la guerra.

53 Pour un conseil écoute
l'homme âgé.

Consejo, tómalo del hombre
viejo.

Die Ansicht eines Weisen und
den Rat eines Greisen soll
man nicht von sich weisen.

Chiedi consiglio a chi è
vecchio.

54 Je ne vends pas la peau de l'ours avant de l'avoir tué.

Man darf niemals die Haut eines Bären verkaufen, bevor man ihn erlegt hat.

Me reparto la piel del oso antes de cazarlo.

Non vendere la pelle dell'orso prima d'averlo preso.

55 La vérité est dans le vin.   Im Wein ist Wahrheit.

En el vino está la verdad.   'In vino veritas' (lat.)

56 Il y a plus de bonheur à donner qu'à recevoir.

Más bienaventurada cosa es dar que recibir.

Geben ist seliger denn nehmen.

Si prova più gioia a dare che a ricevere.

57 On ne se bat pas pour un os.

No es bueno pelear por un hueso.

Sie streiten um des Kaisers Bart.

Non val la pena di litigare per un osso.

58 Il ne faut pas réveiller le chat qui dort.

No hay que buscar tres pies al gato.

Schlafende Hunde soll man nicht wecken.

Non svegliare il can che dorme.

59 La vie passe, l'art demeure.

Die Kunst ist lang, und kurz
ist unser Leben.

El arte es largo y la vida breve.

La vita è breve, l'arte è lunga.

60 Tel père, tel fils; telle mère, telle fille.

De tal palo, tal astilla.

Wie der Vater, so der Sohn; wie die Mutter, so die Tochter.

Tale il padre, tale il figlio; tale la madre, tale la figlia.

61 A telle dame, telle chambrière. Wie die Frau, so die Magd.

A tal dama, tal criada. Tale la padrona, tale la serva.

62 Il faut manger pour vivre et non pas vivre pour manger.

No hay que vivir para comer, sino comer para vivir.

Man lebt nicht, um zu essen, man ißt, um zu leben.

Si deve mangiare per vivere, non vivere per mangiare.

63 Il faut y regarder à deux fois avant de sauter.

Mirar antes de saltar.

Vorm Beginnen sich besinnen, macht gewinnen.

Bisogna pensarci prima per non pentirsi poi.

64 Qui m'aime, aime mon chien.

Quien quiere a Beltrán,
quiere a su can.

Wer die Kirschen will, muß
auch die Steine nehmen.

Chi ama me, ama il mio cane.

65 Aimez votre voisin, mais
ne coupez pas votre haie.

Ama tu vecino pero no
deshagas tu seto.

Liebe Deinen Nachbarn, aber
reiß den Zaun nicht ein.

Vicinanza senza siepe porta
inimicizia in casa.

66 Récolte le blé quand il est mûr.

Im Regen ist schlecht heuen.

Mientras hace calor se pelan los árboles.

Bisogna tagliare il fieno finché non piove.

67 C'est en faisant des fautes qu'on apprend.

Aus Fehlern lernt man.

El errar es maestro del acertar.

Sbagliando s'impara.

68 L'argent appelle l'argent.

Dinero llama a dinero.

Geld kommt zu Geld.

I soldi chiamano soldi.

69 L'avarice est la source de tous les maux.

La avaricia es la raíz de todos los males.

Geld ist die Wurzel allen Übels.

L'avarizia è la radice di tutti i mali.

70 L'argent ouvre toutes les portes.

Geld regiert die Welt.

El dinero abre todas las puertas.

Il denaro apre tutte le porte.

71 Trop grande hâte est cause de retard.

Eile mit Weile.

Vísteme despacio, que tengo prisa.

La troppa fretta spesso causa ritardo.

72 Pour faire un civet, il faut tuer un lièvre.

No le llames grano hasta que esté encerrado.

Ungefangene Fische kann man nicht braten.

Non dire quattro se non l'hai nel sacco.

73 Ne remets jamais à demain ce que tu peux faire aujourd'hui.

Was Du heute kannst besorgen, das verschiebe nicht auf morgen.

No dejes para mañana lo que puedes hacer hoy.

Non rimandare a domani quel che potresti fare oggi.

74 On ne peut pas voler un homme nu.

Einem nackten Mann kann man nicht in die Tasche greifen.

Desnudo nací, desnudo me hallo, ni pierdo ni gano.

Cento ladri non possono spogliare un uomo nudo.

75 On n'est jamais trop vieux pour apprendre.

Man ist nie zu alt zum Lernen.

Nunca es tarde para aprender.

Non si è mai troppo vecchi per imparare.

76 Rien ne vaut un balai neuf.

Escoba nueva barre bien.

Neue Besen kehren gut.

Scopa nuova scopa bene.

77 La nuit porte conseil.   Guter Rat kommt über Nacht.

La noche trae consejo.   La notte porta consiglio.

78 Pas de nouvelles, bonnes nouvelles.

Ninguna nueva, buenas nuevas.

Keine Nachricht, gute Nachricht.

Nessuna nuova, buona nuova.

79 Il n'y a pas de rose sans épines.

Keine Rose ohne Dornen.

No hay rosa sin espinas.

Non c'è rosa senza spine.

80 Il n'est pire aveugle que celui qui ne veut pas voir.

Keiner ist so blind wie derjenige, der nicht sehen will.

No hay peor ciego que el que no quiere ver.

Non c'è peggior cieco di chi non vuol vedere.

81 Il n'est pire sourd que celui
qui ne veut pas entendre.

No hay peor sordo que el que
no quiere oír.

Keiner ist so taub, wie
derjenige, der nicht hören will.

Non c'è peggior sordo di chi
non vuol sentire.

82 On revient toujours à ses premières amours.

Alte Liebe rostet nicht.

El primer amor es el último en olvidarse.

Il primo amore non si scorda mai.

83 Vieillir c'est redevenir enfants.

Die Alten werden zweimal Kinder.

La vejez tornó por los días en que nació.

I vecchi son due volte fanciulli.

84 On ne peut pas faire d'omelettes sans casser des oeufs.

No se hacen tortillas sin huevos.

Wo gehobelt wird, fallen Späne.

Non si fanno frittate senza rompere uova.

85 Un service en vaut un autre.

Un favor se paga con otro.

Eine Gefälligkeit ist der andern wert.

A un favore si risponde con un altro favore.

86 Il faut laver son linge sale en famille.

Man soll schmutzige Wäsche nicht in der Öffentlichkeit waschen.

Los trapos sucios se lavan en casa.

I panni sporchi si lavano in casa.

87 L'un sème, l'autre récolte.

Hay quien siembra y quien cosecha.

Die einen säen, und die anderen ernten.

C'è chi semina e c'è chi raccoglie.

88 Une hirondelle ne fait pas le printemps.

Una golondrina no hace verano.

Eine Schwalbe macht noch keinen Sommer.

Una rondine non fa primavera.

89 L'occasion fait le larron.   Gelegenheit macht Diebe.

La ocasión hace al ladrón.   L'occasione fa l'uomo ladro.

90 Autres temps, autres moeurs.

A otros tiempos, otras costumbres.

Andere Zeiten, andere Sitten.

Altri tempi, altri costumi.

91 Loin des yeux, loin du coeur.   Aus den Augen, aus dem Sinn.

Ojos que no ven, corazón que   Lontano dagli occhi, lontano
no siente.   dal cuore.

92 Il a des dettes par dessus la tête.

Deber a todo el mundo.

Die Schulden wachsen ihm über den Kopf.

Ha debiti fin sopra i capelli.

93 La patience vient à bout de tout.

Con la paciencia todo se alcanza.

Beharrlichkeit führt zum Ziel.

Con la pazienza si ottiene tutto.

94 Médecin, guéris-toi toi-même.   Arzt, hilf Dir selbst.

Médico, cúrate a ti mismo.   Medico, cura te stesso.

95 C'est en forgeant qu'on devient forgeron.

Übung macht den Meister.

El ejercicio hace maestro.

È con l'esercizio che si diventa maestri.

96 Prévenir vaut mieux que guérir.

Vorbeugen ist besser als heilen.

Más vale prevenir que curar.

Meglio prevenire che reprimere.

97 Les rats quittent le navire qui coule.

Las ratas abandonan el barco que se hunde.

Die Ratten verlassen das sinkende Schiff.

I topi abbandonano la nave che affonda.

98 Le vieil arbre transplanté meurt.

Viejas plantas traspuestas, ni crecen ni medran.

Alte Bäume soll man nicht verpflanzen.

Trapianta un albero vecchio, e lo vedrai morire.

99 Passez-moi la rhubarbe, je vous passerai le séné.

Hoy por ti, mañana por mi

Hilfst Du mir, so helf ich Dir.

Io dò una mano a te, tu dai una mano a me.

100 La deuxième idée est la meilleure.

Los segundos pensamientos son los mejores.

Erst wägen, dann wagen.

La seconda idea è sempre la migliore.

101 Voir c'est croire.

Ver es creer.

Was die Augen sehen, glaubt
das Herz.

Quel che l'occhio vede,
il cuore crede.

102 Les cordonniers sont les plus mal chaussés.

Der Schuster trägt die schlechtesten Schuhe.

En casa del herrero, cuchara de palo.

Il calzolaio ha le scarpe rotte.

103 Qui ne dit mot, consent.

Quien calla, otorga.

Wer schweigt, stimmt zu.

Chi tace, acconsente.

104 A renard endormi rien ne tombe dans la gueule.

A la vulpeja dormida no le cae nada en la boca.

Ohne Fleiß kein Preis.

Chi dorme, non piglia pesci.

105 La parole est d'argent,
le silence est d'or.

Reden ist Silber, Schweigen
ist Gold.

La palabra es de plata,
el silencio es de oro.

La parola è d'argento,
il silenzio è d'oro.

106 Il faut battre le fer pendant qu'il est chaud.

Al hierro caliente, batir de repente.

Das Eisen muß man schmieden, solange es heiß ist.

Bisogna battere il ferro finché è caldo.

107 Que chacun balaie devant sa porte.

Cada cual en su casa y Dios en la de todos.

Jeder soll vor seiner eigenen Türe kehren.

Non ficcare il naso negli affari altrui.

108 Chacun ses goûts.

Über Geschmack läßt sich
nicht streiten.

Sobre gustos no hay nada
escrito.

Ognuno ha i suoi gusti.

109 Dis-moi qui tu hantes et je te dirai qui tu es.

Dime con quien andas y te diré quien eres.

Sage mir, mit wem Du umgehst, und ich sage Dir, wer Du bist.

Dimmi con chi vai, e ti dirò chi sei.

110 Chaque troupeau a sa brebis galeuse.

En cada rebaño hay una oveja descarriada.

Überall gibt es schwarze Schafe.

In ogni gregge c'è una pecora nera.

111 La patience a des limites.

La paciencia tiene un límite.

Auch Geduld hat Grenzen.

Anche la pazienza ha un limite.

112 Tout a déjà été dit.

No hay nada que no esté ya
dicho.

Alles ist schon einmal da
gewesen.

Non c'è niente che non sia
già stato detto.

113 Il y a un temps pour parler et un temps pour se taire.

Hay un tiempo para hablar y un tiempo para callar.

Reden hat seine Zeit, und Schweigen hat seine Zeit.

C'è un tempo per parlare e un tempo per tacere.

114 Bienvenu qui apporte.

Los dones cautivan hasta a los dioses.

Wer bringt, ist überall willkommen.

Chi porta, è sempre il benvenuto.

115 Trop de cuisiniers gâtent le potage (ou, la sauce).

Muchos componedores descomponen la novia.

Viele Köche verderben den Brei.

Troppi cuochi rovinano la minestra.

116 L'union fait la force.

La unión hace la fuerza.

Einigkeit macht stark.

L'unione fa la forza.

117 Les murs ont des oreilles.   Wände haben Ohren.

Las paredes oyen.   I muri hanno orecchi.

118 Il faut laisser aller le monde comme il va.

Man muß die Menschen nehmen, wie sie sind.

Tomemos las cosas como vienen.

Bisogna prendere il mondo come viene.

119 Un travail bien commencé est déjà à moitié fait.

Frisch begonnen, ist halb gewonnen.

Quien bien empieza, bien acaba.

Chi ben comincia, è a metà dell'opra.

WHEN A THING IS DONE, ADVICE COMES TOO LATE

120 A parti pris, point de conseil.

Hecho el hecho, huelga el consejo.

Rat nach der ', spät.

Dopo il fatto, il consiglio non vale.

121 Quand tu seras à Rome, agis comme les Romains.

Andere Länder, andere Sitten.

Cuando a Roma fueres, haz como vieres.

Quando a Roma andrai, fa' come vedrai.

122 Quand la pauvreté frappe à la porte, l'amour s'en va par la fenêtre.

Wenn die Not an die Türe klopft, springt die Liebe aus dem Fenster.

Cuando el hambre entra por la puerta, el amor huye por la ventana.

Quando la fame entra dalla porta, l'amore se ne va dalla finestra.

123 Quand le chat n'est pas là, les souris dansent.

Wenn die Katze aus dem Haus ist, tanzen die Mäuse auf dem Tisch.

Cuando el gato no está, los ratones bailan.

Quando non c'è il gatto, i topi ballano.

124 Vouloir c'est pouvoir.

Querer es poder.

Wo ein Wille ist, ist auch ein Weg.

Volere è potere.

125 Celui qui se marie fait bien, celui qui ne se marie pas fait mieux.

El que se casa hace bien, y el que no se casa hace mejor.

Heiraten ist gut, ledig bleiben ist besser.

Chi si sposa fa bene, chi non si sposa fa meglio.

126 Les grands diseurs ne sont pas les grands faiseurs.

Perro ladrador, poco mordedor.

Die Faulen und die Dreisten schreien am meisten.

Chi parla molto, agisce poco.

127 Le loup qui s'est fait agneau.   Ein Wolf im Schafspelz.

Un lobo con piel de oveja.   Un lupo travestito da agnello.

128 Bon cheval, mauvais cheval veut l'éperon; bonne femme, mauvaise femme veut le bâton.

Ein Weib, ein Esel und eine Nuß, diese drei man klopfen muß.

El asno y la mujer, a palos se han de vencer.

Donne, asini e noci voglion le mani atroci.

INDEX

Everyone has a sprinkling of proverbs at the back of the mind, but not everyone can bring out the right one at the right moment. What, for instance, do good parents say to children who are unwilling to do their homework? *Never put off till tomorrow what can be done today.*

"Today" and "tomorrow" are among the key words which appear in this index, together with the relevant number, to a proverb that every child — and grown-up — should know. But "today" and "tomorrow" also come into the saying: *Better an egg today than a hen tomorrow.* For this reason they have more than one page reference, and so does "egg", with the reminder that *omelets are not made without breaking eggs,* in other words you sometimes have to sacrifice one thing in order to achieve your aim.

And what if one has the feeling that there must be a saying to suit a given situation but cannot think of the significant word? In that event we suggest that you look through the index until you come to a word that jogs your memory and then turn to it. You can do so in English, French, German, Spanish and Italian, and if that does not provide you with the proverb you want, we ask your forgiveness. The indexes list 128 proverbs under their key words, whatever part of speech they are: as our artist Silvia Mondini said, *"enough is as good as a feast"*.

ACCUSE: He who excuses himself accuses himself [46].

ADVICE: If you wish good advice, consult an old man [53]; When a thing is done, advice comes too late [120].

ALONE: Better alone than in bad company [7].

ARMED: He's armed to the teeth! [37].

ART: Life is short, but art lives on [59].

ASK: Ask much to have a little [5].

AWAY: When the cat is away the mice will play [123].

BAD: Better alone than in bad company [7].

BARE-FOOT: A shoemaker's wife goes bare-foot [102].

BEAR: I'll sell the bear's skin before I've caught the bear [54].

BEAT: A woman, a dog and a walnut tree, the more you beat them, the better they'll be [128].

BEAUTY: Beauty is skin-deep [6].

BED: As you make your bed, so you must lie on it [4].

BEFORE: There is nothing said which has not been said before [112].

BEGIN: Well begun, is half done [119].

BELIEVE: Seeing is believing [101].

BELLY: The eye is bigger than the belly [23].

BIRD: Birds of a feather flock together [12].

BLACK: There are black sheep in every flock [110].

BLESSED: It is more blessed to give than to receive [56].

BLIND: None so blind as those who won't see [80].

BONE: It's no use fighting over a bone! [57].

BREAK: Omelets are not made without breaking eggs [84].

BRING: Those who bring are always welcome [114].

BROOM: A new broom sweeps clean [76].

BROTH: Every cook praises his own broth [22]; Too many cooks spoil the broth [115].

BUSINESS: Business is business [13].

BUY: He that buys what he does not want, must often sell what he does want [43].

CARE: Care killed the cat [16].

CAT: Care killed the cat [16]; A cat may look at a king [17]; When the cat is away the mice will play [123].

CATCH: I'll sell the bear's skin before I've caught the bear [54]; Never fry a fish till it's caught [72]; The sleeping fox catches no poultry [104].

CHARITY: Charity begins at home [18].

CHILD: The child says nothing, but what he heard at the fireplace [19]; Old men are twice children [83].

CHURCH: All are not saints that go to church [1].

CLEAN: A new broom sweeps clean [76].

CLOTHING: A wolf in sheep's clothing [127].

COLD: A cold hand and a warm heart [20].

COME: First come, first served [26].

COMPANY: Better alone than in bad company [7].

COMPARISON: Comparisons are odious [21].

CONSENT: Silence gives consent [103].

CONSULT: If you wish good advice, consult an old man [53].

CONTEMPT: Familiarity breeds contempt [24].

COOK: Every cook praises his own broth [22]; Too many cooks spoil the broth [115].

COUNSEL: Night is mother of counsel [77].

COUNTRY: God made the country and man made the town [30].

CURE: Prevention is better than cure [96].

DAUGHTER: Like father, like son; like mother, like daughter [60].

DAY: Patient men win the day [93].

DEAF: None so deaf as those who won't hear [81].

DEBT: Over head and ears in debt [92].

DESERVE: One good turn deserves another [85].

DIE: Call no man happy till he dies [15].

DIFFER: Tastes differ [108].

DISH: Better are small fish than an empty dish [9].

DO: By doing nothing we do ill [14]; Well begun, is half done [119]; When a thing is done, advice comes too late [120]; When in Rome do as the Romans do [121]; Who talks most does least [126].

DOG: He that lies down with dogs must rise up with fleas [44]; Let sleeping dogs lie [58]; Love me, love my dog [64]; A woman, a dog and a walnut tree, the more you beat them, the better they'll be [128].

DOOR: Money opens all doors [70]; Sweep before your own door [107]; When poverty comes in at the door, love jumps out of the window [122].

DRAW: Money draws money [68].

EAR: He's put a flea in my ear [41]; Over head and ears in debt [92]; Walls have ears [117].

EAT: Live not to eat, but eat to live [62].

EGG: Better an egg today than a hen tomorrow [8]; Omelets are not made without breaking eggs [84].

EMBROIDERY: Better go to heaven in rags than hell in embroidery [10].

EMPTY: Better are small fish than an empty dish [9].

END: All's well that ends well [2].

EVIL: Money is the root of all evil [69].

EXCUSE: He who excuses himself, accuses himself [46].

EYE: The eye is bigger than the belly [23]; Four eyes see more than two [28].

FAMILIARITY: Familiarity breeds contempt [24].

FATHER: Like father, like son; like mother, like daughter [60].

FEATHER: Birds of a feather flock together [12].

FIGHT: It's no use fighting over a bone! [57].

FIND: He who seeks will find [47]; We must take the world as we find it [118].

FIRE. Fire and water are good servants, but bad masters [25].

FIREPLACE: The child says nothing, but what he heard at the fireplace [19].

FIRST: First come, first served [26].

FISH: Better are small fish than an empty dish [9]; Never fry a fish till it's caught [72].

FLEA: He's put a flea in my ear [41]; He that lies down with dogs must rise up with fleas [44].

FLOCK (noun): There are black sheep in every flock [110].

FLOCK (verb): Birds of a feather flock together [12].

FOOL: A fool and his money are soon parted [27].

FOOT: He has one foot in the grave [38].

FORGET: Old love will not be forgotten [82].

FOUR: Four eyes see more than two [28].

FOX: The sleeping fox catches no poultry [104.

FRENCH: He's taken French leave [42].

FRIEND: Tell me who your friends are and I'll tell you what you are [109].

FRY: Never fry a fish till it's caught [72].

GARMENT: The garment makes the man [29].

GIVE: It is more blessed to give than to receive [56].

GO: All are not saints that go to church [1].

GOD: God made the country and man made the town [30].

GOLDEN: Speech is silver, but silence is golden [105].

GOOD: A good horse should seldom be spurred [31]; No news is good news [78]; One good turn deserves another [85].

GRAVE: He has one foot in the grave [38].

HABIT: Habit is almost second nature [33].

HALF: Well begun, is half done [119].

HAND: A cold hand and a warm heart [20].

HAPPY: Call no man happy till he dies [15].

HASTE: Haste makes waste [34]; More haste less speed [71].

HAY: Make hay while the sun shines [66].

HEAD: Over head and ears in debt [92].

HEAL: Physician, heal thyself [94].

HEALTH: Health is better than wealth [35].

HEAR: The child says nothing, but what he heard at the fireplace [19]; None so deaf as those who won't hear [81].

HEART: A cold hand and a warm heart [20].

HEAVEN: Better go to heaven in rags than hell in embroidery [10].

HEDGE: Love your neighbour, yet don't pull down your hedge [65].

HELL: Better go to heaven in rags than hell in embroidery [10].

HEN: Better an egg today than a hen tomorrow [8].

HOME: Charity begins at home [18].

HONESTY: Honesty is the best policy [49].

HORSE: A good horse should seldom be spurred [31].

HOT: Strike while the iron is hot [106].

HOUSE: The house shows the owner [50].

HUNGER: Hunger is the best sauce [51].

ILL: By doing nothing we do ill [14].

IRON: Strike while the iron is hot [106].

JUICE: He'll stew in his own juice [36].

KILL: Care killed the cat [16].

KING: A cat may look at a king [17].

KNOW: He who travels far knows much [48].

LATE: Better late than never [11]; When a thing is done, advice comes too late [120].

LEAD: He's leading me by my nose! [39].

LEAP: Look before you leap [63].

LEARN: Never too old to learn [75].

LEAST: Who talks most does least [126].

LEAVE (noun): He's taken French leave [42].

LEAVE (verb.): Rats leave a sinking ship [97].

LIBERTY: He that marries for wealth, sells his liberty [45].

LIE: As you make your bed, so you must lie on it [4]; He that lies down with dogs must rise up with fleas [44]; Let sleeping dogs lie [58].

LIFE: Life is short, but art lives on [59].

LIMIT: There is a limit to one's patience [111].

LINEN: One should not wash one's dirty linen in public [86].

LITTLE: Ask much to have a little [5].

LIVE: Live not to eat, but eat to live [62].

LOG: Roll my log, and I'll roll yours [99].

LOOK: A cat may look at a king [17]; Look before you leap [63].

LOVE (noun): Old love will not be forgotten [82]; When poverty comes in at the door, love jumps out of the window [122].

LOVE (verb): Love me, love my dog [64]; Love your neighbour, yet don't pull down your hedge [65].

MAID: Like mistress, like maid [61].

MAKE: As you make your bed, so you must lie on it [4]; Omelets are not made without breaking eggs [84]; One swallow does not make a summer [88]; Opportunity makes the thief [89]; Practice makes perfect [95].

MAN: Call no man happy till he dies [15]; The garment makes the man [29]; God made the country and man made the town [30]; If you wish good advice, consult an old man [53]; Never rob naked men [74]; Old men are twice children [83]; Patient men win the day [93].

MANNER: Other times, other manners [90].

MARRY: He that marries for wealth, sells his liberty [45]; Who marries does well, who marries not does better [125].

MASTER: Fire and water are good servants, but bad masters [25].

MIND: Out of sight, out of mind [91].

MISTAKE: Mistakes are often the best teachers [67].

MISTRESS: Like mistress, like maid [61].

MONEY: A fool and his money are soon parted [27]; Money draws money [68]; Money is the root of all evil [69]; Money opens all doors [70].

MOTHER: Like father, like son; like mother, like daughter [60]; Night is mother of counsel [77].

MOUSE: When the cat is away the mice will play [123].

NAKED: Never rob naked men [74].

NATURE: Habit is almost second nature [33].

NEEDLE: He's on pins and needles [40].

NEIGHBOUR: Love your neighbour, yet don't pull down your hedge [65].

NEVER: Better late than never [11].

NEW: A new broom sweeps clean [76].

NEWS: No news is good news [78].

NIGHT: Night is mother of counsel [77].

NOSE: He's leading me by my nose! [39].

NOTHING: By doing nothing we do ill [14]; The child says nothing, but what he heard at the fireplace [19]; When poverty comes in at the door, love jumps out of the window [112].

OLD: If you wish good advice, consult an old man [53]; Never too old to learn [75]; Old love will not be forgotten [82]; Old men are twice children [83]; Remove an old tree, and it will wither to death [98].

OMELET: Omelets are not made without breaking eggs [84].

OPPORTUNITY: Opportunity makes the thief [89].

OWNER: The house shows the owner [50].

PART: A fool and his money are soon parted [27].

PATIENCE: There is a limit to one's patience [111].

PATIENT: Patient men win the day [93].

PAY: As the work, so the pay [3].

PEACE: If you wish for peace, be prepared for war [52].

PERFECT: Practice makes perfect [95].

PHYSICIAN: Physician, heal thyself [94].

PIN: He's on pins and needles [40].

PLAY: When the cat is away the mice will play [123].

PLEASURE: The great source of pleasure is variety [32].

POLICY: Honesty is the best policy [49].

POULTRY: The sleeping fox catches no poultry [104].

POVERTY: When poverty comes in at the door, love jumps out of the window [122].

PRACTICE: Practice makes perfect [95].

PRAISE: Every cook praises his own broth [22].

PREVENTION: Prevention is better than cure [96].

PUBLIC: One should not wash one's dirty linen in public [86].

RAG: Better go heaven in rags than hell in embroidery [10].

RAT: Rats leave a sinking ship [97].

REAP: One sows and another reaps [87].

RECEIVE: It is more blessed to give than to receive [56].

REMOVE: Remove an old tree, and it will wither to death [98].

RISE: He that lies down with dogs must rise up with fleas [44].

ROB: Never rob naked men [74].

ROLL: Roll my log, and I'll roll yours [99].

ROME: When in Rome do as the Romans do [121].

ROOT: Money is the root of all evil [69].

ROSE: No rose without thorns [79].

SAINT: All are not saints that go to church [1].

SAUCE: Hunger is the best sauce [51].

SAY: There is nothing said which has not been said before [112].

SECOND: Second thoughts are best [100].

SEE: Four eyes see more than two [28]; None so blind as those who won't see [80]; Seeing is believing [101].

SEEK: He who seeks will find [47].

SELL: He that buys what he does not want, must often sell what he does want [43]; He that marries for wealth, sells his liberty [45]; I'll sell the bear's skin before I've caught the bear [54].

SERVANT: Fire and water are good servants, but bad masters [25].

SERVE: First come, first served [26].

SHEEP: There are black sheep in every flock [110]; A wolf in sheep's clothing [127].

SHIP: Rats leave a sinking ship [97].

SHOEMAKER: A shoemaker's wife goes bare-foot [102].

SIGHT: Out of sight, out of mind [91].

SILENCE: Silence gives consent [103]; Speech is silver, but silence is golden [105].

SILENT: There is a time to speak and a time to be silent [113].

SILVER: Speech is silver, but silence is golden [105].

SLEEPING: Let sleeping dogs lie [58]; The sleeping fox catches no poultry [104].

SMALL: Better are small fish than an empty dish [9].

SON: Like father, like son; like mother, like daughter [60].

SOW: One sows and another reaps [87].

SPEAK: There is a time to speak and a time to be silent [113].

SPEECH: Speech is silver, but silence is golden [105].

SPEED: More haste less speed [71];

SPOIL: Too many cooks spoil the broth [115].

SPUR: A good horse should seldom be spurred [31].

STEW: He'll stew in his own juice [36].

STRENGTH: Union is strength [116].

STRIKE: Strike while the iron is hot [106].

SUMMER: One swallow does not make a summer [88].

SUN: Make hay while the sun shines [66].

SWALLOW: One swallow does not make a summer [88].

SWEEP: A new broom sweeps clean [76]; Sweep before your own door [107].

TALK: Who talks most does least [126].

TASTE: Tastes differ [108].

TEACHER: Mistakes are often the best teachers [67].

TELL: Tell me who your friends are and I'll tell you what you are [109].

THIEF: Opportunity makes the thief [89].

THORN: No rose without thorns [79].

THOUGHT: Second thoughts are best [100].

TIME: Other times, other manners [90]; There is a time to speak and a time to be silent [113].

TODAY: Better an egg today than a hen tommorroy [8]; Never put off till tomorrow what may be done today [73].

TOMORROW: Better an egg today than a hen tomorrow [8]; Never put off till tomorrow what may be done today [73].

TOOTH: He's armed to the teeth! [37].

TOWN: God made the country and man made the town [30].

TRAVEL: He who travels far knows much [48].

TREE: Remove an old tree, and it will wither to death [98].

TRUTH: In wine there is truth [55].

TURN: One good turn deserves another [85].

UNION: Union is strength [116].

VARIETY: The great source of pleasure is variety [32].

WALL: Walls have ears [117].

WALNUT TREE: A woman, a dog and a walnut tree, the more you beat them, the better they'll be [128].

WANT: He that buys what he does not want, must often sell what he does want [43].

WAR: If you wish for peace, be prepared for war [52].

WARM: A cold hand and a warm heart [20].

WASH: One should not wash one's dirty linen in public [86].

WASTE: Haste makes waste [34].

WATER: Fire and water are good servants, but bad masters [25].

WAY: Where there's a will, there's a way [124].

WEALTH: Health is better than wealth [35]; He that marries for wealth, sells his liberty [45].

WELCOME: Those who bring are always welcome [114].

WELL: All's well that ends well [2]; Well begun, is half done [119]; Who marries does well, who marries not does better [125].

WILL: Where there's a will, there's a way [124].

WIN: Patient men win the day [93].

WINDOW: When poverty comes in at the door, love jumps out of the window [122].

WINE: In wine there is truth [55].

WITHER: Remove an old tree, and it will wither to death [98].

WOLF: A wolf in sheep's clothing [127].

WOMAN: A woman, a dog and a walnut tree, the more you beat them, the better they'll be [128].

WORK: As the work, so the pay [3].

WORLD: We must take the world as we find it [118].

ACCUSER (s'): Qui s'excuse s'accuse [46].

ACHETER: Qui achète ce dont il n'a pas besoin devra vendre ce qu'il ne voudrait pas [43].

AFFAIRE: Les affaires sont les affaires [13].

AGE: Pour un conseil écoute l'homme âgé [53].

AGIR: Quand tu seras à Rome, agis comme les Romains [121].

AGNEAU: Le loup qui s'est fait agneau [127].

AIMER: Qui m'aime, aime mon chien [64];
Aimez votre voisin mais ne coupez pas votre haie [65].

ALLER: Il faut laisser aller le monde comme il va [118].

AMOUR: On revient toujours à ses premières amours [82];
Quand la pauvreté frappe à la porte, l'amour s'en va par la fenêtre [122].

ANGLAIS: Il a filé à l'anglaise [42].

APPELER: L'argent appelle l'argent [68].

APPETIT: Il n'est sauce que d'appétit [51].

APPORTER: Bienvenu qui apporte [114].

APPRENDRE: C'est en faisant des fautes qu'on apprend [67];
On n'est jamais trop vieux pour apprendre [75].

ARBRE: Le vieil arbre transplanté meurt [98].

ARGENT: Le fou et son argent sont bientôt séparés [27];
En épousant sa femme pour son argent, il a vendu sa liberté [45]; L'argent appelle l'argent [68]; L'argent ouvre toutes les portes [70]; La parole est d'argent, le silence est d'or [105].

ARMER: Il est armé de pied en cap [37].

ARRIVER: Premier arrivé, premier servi [26].

ART: La vie passe, l'art demeure [59].

ASSEMBLER (s'): Qui se ressemble s'assemble [12].

ASSIETTE: Petite friture vaut mieux qu'assiette vide [9].

AUJOURD'HUI: Mieux vaut un oeuf aujourd'hui qu'une poule demain [8]; Ne remets jamais à demain ce que tu peux faire aujourd'hui [73].

AUTRE: Un service en vaut un autre [85]; Autres temps, autres moeurs [90].

AVARICE: L'avarice est la source de tous les maux [69].

AVEUGLE: Il n'est pire aveugle que celui qui ne veut pas voir [80].

BALAI: Rien ne vaut un balai neuf [76].

BALAYER: Que chacun balaie devant sa porte [107].

BATTRE: On ne se bat pas pour un os [57]; Il faut battre le fer pendant qu'il est chaud [106].

BEAUTE: La beauté est éphémère [6].

BESOIN: Bon cheval n'a pas besoin d'éperon [31]; Qui achète ce dont il n'a pas besoin devra vendre ce qu'il ne voudrait pas [43].

BIEN: Tout est bien qui finit bien [2].

BIENVENU: Bienvenu qui apporte [114].

BLANCHIR: Les soucis font blanchir les cheveux de bonne heure [16].

BLE: Récolte le blé quand il est mûr [66].

BON: Bon cheval n'a pas besoin d'éperon [30]; Pas de nouvelles, bonnes nouvelles [78].

BONHEUR: Il y a plus de bonheur à donner qu'à recevoir [56].

BOUT: Il me mène par le bout du nez [39]; La patience vient à bout de tout [93].

BREBIS: Chaque troupeau a sa brebis galeuse [110].

CAMPAGNE: Dieu fit la campagne, l'homme fit la ville [30].

CAP: Il est armé de pied en cap [37].

CASSER: On ne peut pas faire d'omelette sans casser des oeufs [84].

CAUSE: Trop grande hâte est cause de retard [71].

CHACUN: Que chacun balaie devant sa porte [107; Chacun ses goûts [108].

CHAMBRIERE: A telle dame, telle chambrière [61].

CHARITE: Charité bien ordonnée commence par soi-même [18].

CHAT: Il ne faut pas réveiller le chat qui dort [58]; Quand le chat n'est pas là, les souris dansent [123].

CHAUD: A main froide, coeur chaud [20]; Il faut battre le fer pendant qu'il est chaud [106].

CHAUSSER: Les cordonniers sont les plus mal chaussés [102].

CHERCHER: Qui cherche trouve [47].

CHEVAL: Bon cheval n'a pas besoin d'éperon [31].

CHEVEU: Les soucis font blanchir les cheveux de bonne heure [16].

CHIEN: Un chien regarde bien un évêque [17]; Qui se couche avec des chiens se lève avec des puces [44]; Il ne faut pas réveiller le chien qui dort [58]; Qui m'aime, aime mon chien [64].

CIVET: Pour faire un civet, il faut tuer un lièvre [72].

COEUR: A main froide, coeur chaud [20]; Loin des yeux, loin du coeur [91].

COMMENCER: Charité bien ordonnée commence par soi-même [18]; Un travail bien commencé est déjà à moitié fait [119].

COMPAGNIE: Mieux vaut être seul qu'en mauvaise compagnie [7].

COMPARAISON: Comparaison n'est pas raison [21].

CONNAÎTRE: Le maison fait connaître le maître [50]; Ce que l'enfant entend au foyer est bientôt connu jusqu'au moustier [19].

CONSEIL: La nuit porte conseil [77]; Pour un conseil écoute l'homme âgé [53]; A parti pris, point de conseil [120].

CONSENTIR: Qui ne dit mot, consent [103].

CORDONNIER: Les cordonniers sont les plus mal chaussés [102].

COUCHER (se): Comme on fait son lit, on se couche [4]; Qui se couche avec des chiens se lève avec des puces [44].

COULER: Les rats quittent le navire qui coule [97].

COUPER: Aimez votre voisin mais ne coupez pas votre haie [65].

CROIRE: Voir c'est croire [101].

CUIRE: Il cuit dans son jus [36].

CUISINIER: Trop de cuisiniers gâtent le potage [115].

DAME: A telle dame, telle chambrière [61].

DANSER: Quand le chat n'est pas là, les souris dansent [123].

DEMAIN: Mieux vaut un oeuf aujourd'hui qu'une poule demain [8]; Ne remets jamais à demain ce que tu peux faire aujourd'hui [73].

DEMANDER: Demande beaucoup pour avoir un peu [5].

DEMEURER: La vie passe, l'art demeure [59].

DENTELLE: Mieux vaut aller au paradis en haillons qu'en enfer en habit de dentelle [10].

DETTE: Il a des dettes par dessus la tête [92].

DEUXIÈME: La deuxième idée est la meilleure [100].

DEVENIR: C'est en forgeant qu'on devient forgeron [95].

DIEU: Dieu fit la campagne, l'homme fit la ville [30].

DIRE: Qui ne dit mot, consent [103]; Dis-moi qui tu hantes et je te dirai qui tu es [109]; Tout a déjà été dit [112].

DISEUR: Les grands diseurs ne sont pas les grands faiseurs [126].

DIVERSITE: Diversité réjouit [32].

DONNER: Il y a plus de bonheur à donner qu'à recevoir [56].

DORMIR: Il faut pas réveiller le chien qui dort [58].

EAU: Le feu et l'eau sont bons serviteurs mais mauvais maîtres [25].

ECOUTER: Pour un conseil écoute l'homme âgé [53].

EGLISE: Tous ceux qui vont à l'église ne sont pas des saints [1].

ENDORMIR: A renard endormi rien ne tombe dans la gueule [104].

ENFANT: Ce que l'enfant entend au foyer est bientôt connu

jusqu'au moustier [19]; Les enfants répétent ce qu'ils ont entendu [19]; Vieillir c'est redevenir enfants [83].

ENFER: Mieux vaut aller au paradis en haillons qu'en enfer en habit de dentelle [10].

ENGENDRER: La familiarité engendre le mépris [24].

ENTENDRE: Ce que l'enfant entend au foyer est bientôt connu jusqu'au moustier [19]; Il n'est pire sourd que celui qui ne veut pas entendre [81].

EPERON: Bon cheval n'a pas besoin d'éperon [31].

EPHEMERE: La beauté est éphémère [6].

EPINE: Il est sur des épines [40]; Il n'y a pas de rose sans épines [79].

EPOUSER: En épousant sa femme pour son argent, il a vendu sa liberté [45].

EVÊQUE: Un chien regarde bien un évêque [17].

EXCUSER: Qui s'excuse, s'accuse [46].

FAIM: La faim est la meilleure des sauces [51].

FAIRE: Comme on fait son lit, on se couche [4]; C'est en faisant des fautes qu'on apprend [67]; Ne remets jamais à demain ce que tu peux faire aujourd'hui [73]; Une hirondelle ne fait pas le printemps [88]; L'occasion fait le larron [89]; Un travail bien commencé est déjà à moitié fait [119].

FAISEUR: Les grands diseurs ne sont pas les grands faiseurs [126].

FALLOIR: Il faut laver son linge sale en famille [86]; Il faut battre le fer pendant qu'il est chaud [106].

FAMILIARITE: La familiarité engendre le mépris [24].

FAMILLE: Il faut laver son linge sale en famille [86].

FAUTE: Faute de grives on mange des merles [9]; C'est en faisant des fautes qu'on apprend [67].

FEMME: En épousant sa femme pour son argent, il a vendu sa liberté [45].

FENÊTRE: Quand la pauvreté frappe à la porte, l'amour s'en va par la fenêtre [122].

FER: Il faut battre le fer pendant qu'il est chaud [106].

FEU: Le feu et l'eau sont bons serviteurs mais mauvais maîtres [25].

FILER: Il a filé à l'anglaise [42].

FILLE/FILS: Tel père, tel fils; telle mère, telle fille [60].

FINIR: Tout est bien qui finit bien [2].

FOIS: Il faut y regarder à deux fois avant de sauter [63].

FORCE: L'union fait la force [116].

FORGER: C'est en forgeant qu'on devient forgeron [95].

FORGERON: C'est en forgeant qu'on devient forgeron [95].

FOU: Le fou et son argent sont bientôt séparés [27].

FOYER: Ce que l'enfant entend au foyer est bientôt connu jusqu'au moustier [19].

FRAPPER: Quand la pauvreté frappe à la porte, l'amour s'en va par la fenêtre [122].

FRITURE: Petite friture vaut mieux qu'assiette vide [9].

FROID: A main froide, coeur chaud [20].

GALEUX: Chaque troupeau a sa brebis galeuse [110].

GÂTER: Trop de cuisiniers gâtent le potage [115].

GOÛT: Chacun ses goûts [108].

GRAND: Il a les yeux plus grands que le ventre [23].

GRIVE: Faute de grives on mange des merles [9].

GUÉRIR: Médecin, guéris-toi toi-même [94]; Prévenir vaut mieux que guérir [96].
GUERRE: Si tu veux la paix, prépare la guerre [52].

GUEULE: A renard endormi rien ne tombe dans la gueule [104].

GUIDE: L'honnêteté est le meilleur des guides [49].

HABIT: Mieux vaut aller au paradis en haillons qu'en enfer en habit de dentelle [10]; L'habit fait l'homme [29].

HABITUDE: L'habitude est une seconde nature [33].

HAIE: Aimez votre voisin mais ne coupez pas votre haie [65].

HAILLONS: Mieux vaut aller au paradis en haillons qu'en enfer en habit de dentelle [10].

HANTER: Dis-moi qui tu hantes et je te dirai qui tu es [109].

HATE: Trop grande hâte est cause de retard [71].

HEUREUX: Nul avant sa mort ne peut être dit heureux [15].

HIRONDELLE: Une hirondelle ne fait pas le printemps [88].

HOMME: L'habit fait l'homme [29]; Dieu fit la campagne, l'homme fit la ville [30]; Pour un conseil écoute l'homme âgé [53]; On ne peut pas voler un homme nu [74].

HONNÊTETE: L'honnêteté est le meilleur des guides [49].

HONNEUR: Il vaut mieux vivre pauvre qu'injuste et dans les honneurs [10].

IDEE: La deuxième idée est la meilleure [100].

INJUSTE: Il vaut mieux vivre pauvre qu'injuste et dans les honneurs [10].

INSTRUIRE (s'): On s'instruit en voyageant [48].

JAMAIS: Mieux vaut tard que jamais [11]. Ne remets jamais à demain ce que tu peux faire aujourd'hui [73]. On n'est jamais trop vieux pour apprendre [75].

JUS: Il cuit dans son jus [36].

LAISSER: Il faut laisser aller le monde comme il va [118].

LARRON: L'occasion fait le larron [89].

LAVER: Il faut laver son linge sale en famille [86].

LEVER (se): Qui se couche avec des chiens se lève avec des puces [44].

LIBERTE: En épousant sa femme pour son argent, il a vendu sa liberté [45].

LIEVRE: Pour faire un civet, il faut tuer un lièvre [72].

LIMITE: La patience a des limites [111].

LINGE: Il faut laver son linge sale en famille [86].

LIT: Comme on fait son lit, on se couche [4].

LOIN: Loin des yeux, loin du coeur [91].

LOUER: Chacun loue son oeuvre [22].

LOUP: Le loup qui s'est fait agneau [127].

MAIN: A main froide, coeur chaud [20].

MAISON: Les enfants répétent ce qu'ils ont entendu à la maison [19]; La maison fait connaître le maître [50].

MAÎTRE: Le feu et l'eau sont bons serviteurs mais mauvais maîtres [25]; La maison fait connaître le maître [50].

MAL (adv.): Qui ne fait rien fait mal [14].

MAL (subst.): L'avarice est la source de tous les maux [69].

MARIER (se): Celui qui se marie fait bien, celui qui ne se marie pas fait mieux [125].

MANGER: Il faut manger pour vivre et non pas vivre pour manger [62]; Pour manger du poisson, il faut en prendre [72].

MAUVAIS: Mieux vaut être seul qu'en mauvaise compagnie [7]; Le feu et l'eau sont bons serviteurs mais mauvais maîtres [25].

MÉDECIN: Médecin, guéris-toi toi-même [94].

MEILLEUR: L'honnêteté est le meilleur des guides [49]; La faim est la meilleure des sauces [51]; La deuxième idée est la meilleure [100].

MENER: Il me mène par le bout du nez [39].

MÉPRIS: La familiarité engendre le mépris [24].

MÈRE: Tel père, tel fils; telle mère, telle fille [60].

MERLE: Faute de grives, on mange des merles [9].

METTRE: Il m'a mis la puce à l'oreille [41].

MOEURS: Autres temps, autres moeurs [90].

MOITIE: Un travail bien commencé est déjà à moitié fait [119].

MONDE: Il faut laisser aller le monde comme il va [118].

MORT: Nul avant sa mort ne peut être dit heureux [15].

MOT: Qui ne dit mot consent [103].

MOURIR: Le vieil arbre transplanté meurt [98].

MOUSTIER: Ce que l'enfant entend au foyer est bientôt connu jusqu'au moustier [19].

MUR: Les murs ont des oreilles [117].

MÛR: Récolte le blé quand il est mûr [66].

NATURE: L'habitude est une seconde nature [33].

NAVIRE: Les rats quittent le navire qui coule [97].

NEUF: Rien ne vant un balai neuf [76].

NEZ: Il me mène par le bout du nez [39].

NOUVELLE: Pas de nouvelles, bonnes nouvelles [78].

NU: On ne peut voler un homme nu [74].

NUIRE: Trop presser nuit [34].

NUIT: La nuit porte conseil [77].

OCCASION: L'occasion fait le larron [89].

OEIL: Il a les yeux plus grands que le ventre [23]; Quatre yeux voient mieux que deux [28]; Loin des yeux, loin du coeur [91].

OEUF: Mieux vaut un oeuf aujourd'hui qu'une poule demain [8]; On ne peut pas faire d'omelettes sans casser des oeufs [84].

OEUVRE: Chacun loue son oeuvre [22].

OMELETTE: On ne peut faire d'omelettes sans casser des oeufs [84].

OR: La parole est d'argent, le silence est d'or [105].

ORDONNÉ: Charité bien ordonnée commence par soi-même [18].

OREILLE: Il m'a mis la puce à l'oreille [41]; Les murs ont des oreilles [117].

OS: On ne se bat pas pour un os [57].

OURS: Je ne vends pas la peau de l'ours avant de l'avoir tué [54].

OUVRIR: L'argent ouvre toutes les portes [70].

PAIX: Si tu veux la paix, prépare la guerre [52].

PARADIS: Mieux vaut aller au paradis en haillons qu'en enfer en habit de dentelle [10].

PARLER: Il y a un temps pour parler et un temps pour se taire [113].

PAROLE: La parole est d'argent, le silence est d'or [105].

PARTI: A parti pris, point de conseil [120].

PASSER: Santé passe richesse [35]; La vie passe, l'art

demeure [59]; Passez-moi la rhubarbe, je vous passerai le séné [99].

PATIENCE: La patience vient à bout de tout [93]; La patience a des limites [111].

PAUVRE: Il vaut mieux vivre pauvre qu'injuste et dans les honneurs [10].

PAUVRETE: Quand la pauvreté frappe à la porte, l'amour s'en va par la fenêtre [122].

PEAU: Je ne vends pas la peau de l'ours avant de l'avoir tué [54].

PERE: Tel père, tel fils; telle mère, telle fille [60].

PETIT: Petite friture vaut mieux qu'assiette vide [9].

PEU: Demande beaucoup pour avoir un peu [5].

PIED: Il est armé de pied en cap [37]; Il a un pied dans la tombe [38].

PIRE: Il n'est pire aveugle que celui qui ne veut pas voir [80]; Il n'est pire sourd que celui qui ne veut pas entendre [81].

POISSON: Pour manger du poisson, il faut en prendre [72].

PORTE: L'argent ouvre toutes les portes [70]; Que chacun balaie devant sa porte [107]; Quand la pauvreté frappe à la porte, l'amour s'en va par la fenêtre [122].

PORTER: La nuit porte conseil [77].

POTAGE: Trop de cuisiniers gâtent le potage [115].

POULE: Mieux vaut un oeuf aujourd'hui qu'une poule demain [8].

POUVOIR: Ne remets jamais à demain ce que tu peux faire aujourd'hui [73]; On ne peut pas voler un homme nu [74];

On ne peut pas faire d'omelettes sans casser des oeufs [84]; Vouloir c'est pouvoir [124].

PREMIER: Premier arrivé, premier servi [26]; On revient toujours à ses premières amours [82].

PRENDRE: Pour manger du poisson, il faut en prendre [72]; A parti pris point de conseil [120].

PREPARER: Si tu veux la paix, prépare la guerre [52].

PRESSER: Trop presser nuit [34].

PREVENIR: Prévenir vaut mieux que guérir [96].

PRINTEMPS: Une hirondelle ne fait pas le printemps [88].

PUCE: Il m'a mis la puce à l'oreille [41]; Qui se couche avec des chiens se lève avec des puces [44].

QUATRE: Quatre yeux voient mieux que deux [28].

QUITTER: Les rats quittent le navire qui coule [97].

RAISON: Comparaison n'est pas raison [21].

RAT: Les rats quittent le navire qui coulent [97].

RECEVOIR: Il y a plus de bonheur à donner qu'à recevoir [56].

RECOLTER: Récolte le blé quand il est mûr [66]; L'un sème, l'autre récolte [87].

REDEVENIR: Vieillir c'est redevenir enfants [83].

REGARDER: Un chien regarde bien un évêque [17]; Il faut y regarder à deux fois avant de sauter [63].

REJOUIR: Diversité réjouit [32].

REMETTRE: Ne remets jamais à demain ce que tu peux faire aujourd'hui [73].

RENARD: A renard endormi rien ne tombe dans la gueule [104].

REPETER: Les enfants répètent ce qu'ils ont entendu [19].

RESSEMBLER (se): Qui se ressemble s'assemble [12].

RETARD: Trop grande hâte est cause de retard [71].

REVEILLER: Il ne faut pas réveiller le chien qui dort [58].

REVENIR: On revient toujours à ses premières amours [82].

RHUBARBE: Passez-moi la rhubarbe, je vous passerai le séné [99].

RICHESSE: Santé passe richesse [35].

RIEN: Qui ne fait rien fait mal [14].

ROMAIN: Quand tu seras à Rome, agis comme les Romains [121].

ROME: Quand tu seras à Rome, agis comme les Romains [121].

ROSE: Il n'y a pas de rose sans épines [79].

SAINT: Tous ceux qui vont à l'église ne sont pas des saints [1].

SALAIRE: Tel travail, tel salaire [3].

SALE: Il faut laver son linge sale en famille [85]

SANTE: Santé passe richesse [35].

SAUCE: Il n'est sauce que d'appétit [51]; La faim est la meilleure des sauces [51]; Trop de cuisiniers gâtent la sauce [115].

SAUTER: Il faut y regarder à deux fois avant de sauter [63].

SECOND: L'habitude est une seconde nature [33].

SEMER: L'un sème, l'autre récolte [87].

SENE: Passez-moi la rhubarbe, je vous passerai le séné [99].

SEPARER: Le fou et son argent sont bientôt séparés [27].

SERVICE: Un service en vaut un autre [85].

SERVIR: Premier arrivé, premier servi [26].

SERVITEUR: Le feu et l'eau sont bons serviteurs mais mauvais maîtres [25].

SEUL: Mieux vaut être seul qu'en mauvaise compagnie [7].

SILENCE: La parole est d'argent, le silence est d'or [105].

SOUCI: Les soucis font blanchir les cheveux de bonne heure [16].

SOURCE: L'avarice est la source de tous les maux [69].

SOURD: Il n'est pire sourd que celui qui ne veut pas entendre [81].

SOURIS: Quand le chat n'est pas là, les souris dansent [123].

TAIRE (se): Il y a un temps pour parler et un temps pour se taire [113].

TARD: Mieux vaut tard que jamais [11].

TEMPS: Autres temps, autres moeurs [90]; Il y a un temps pour parler et un temps pour se taire [113].
TÊTE: Il a des dettes par dessus la tête [92].

TOMBE: Il a un pied dans la tombe [38].

TOMBER: A renard endormi rien ne tombe dans la gueule [104].

TRANSPLANTER: Le vieil arbre transplanté meurt [98].

TRAVAIL: Tel travail, tel salaire [3]; Un travail bien commencé est déjà à moitié fait [119].

TROUPEAU: Chaque troupeau a sa brebis galeuse [110].

TROUVER: Qui cherche trouve [47].

TUER: Je ne vends pas la peau de l'ours avant de l'avoir tué [54]; Pour faire un civet, il faut tuer un lièvre [72].

UNION: L'union fait la force [116].

VALOIR: Petite friture vaut mieux qu'assiette vide [9]; Rien ne vaut un balai neuf [76]; Un service en vaut un autre [85].

VENDRE: Qui achète ce dont il n'a pas besoin devra vendre ce qu'il ne voudrait pas [43]; En épousant sa femme pour son argent, il a vendu sa liberté [45]; Je ne vends pas la peau de l'ours avant de l'avoir tué [54].

VENTRE: Il a les yeux plus grands que le ventre [23].

VERITE: La vérité est dans le vin [55].

VIDE: Petite friture vaut mieux qu'assiette vide [9].

VIE: La vie passe, l'art demeure [59].

VIEIL: On n'est jamais trop vieux pour apprendre [75]; Le vieil arbre transplanté meurt [98].

VIEILLIR: Vieillir c'est redevenir enfants [83].

VILLE: Dieu fit la campagne, l'homme fit la ville [30].

VIN: La vérité est dans le vin [55].

VIVRE: Il vaut mieux vivre pauvre qu'injuste et dans les honneurs [10]; Il faut manger pour vivre et non pas vivre pour manger [62].

VOIR: Quatre yeux voient mieux que deux [28]; Il n'est pire aveugle que celui qui ne veut pas voir [80]; Voir c'est croire [101].

VOISIN: Aimez votre voisin mais ne coupez pas votre haie [65].

VOLER: On ne peut pas voler un homme nu [74].

VOULOIR: Qui achète ce dont il n'a pas besoin devra vendre ce qu'il ne voudrait pas [43]; Si tu veux la paix, prépare la guerre [52]; Il n'est pire aveugle que celui qui ne veut pas voir [80]; Il n'est pire aveugle que celui qui ne veut pas entendre [81]; Vouloir c'est pouvoir [124].

VOYAGER: On s'instruit en voyageant [48].

YEUX: Il a les yeux plus grands que le ventre [23]; Quatre yeux voient mieux que deux [28]; Loin des yeux, loin du coeur [91].

ABWECHSLUNG: In der Abwechslung liegt das Vergnügen [32].

ALLEIN: Besser allein als in schlechter Gesellschaft [7].

ALLES: Ende gut, alles gut [2]; Alles ist schon einmal da gewesen [112].

ALT: Wie die Alten sungen, so zwitschern auch die Jungen [19]; Man ist nie zu alt zum Lernen [75]; Alte Liebe rostet nicht [82]; Die Alten werden zweimal Kinder [83]; Alte Bäume soll man nicht verpflanzen [98].

ANDER: Eine Gefälligkeit ist der andern wert [85]; Die einen säen, und die anderen ernten [87]; Andere Zeiten, andere Sitten [90]; Andere Länder, andere Sitten [121].

ANFANG: Müßiggang ist aller Laster Anfang [14].

ANKLAGEN: Wer sich entschuldigt, klagt sich an [46].

ANKOMMEN: Auf die inneren Werte kommt es an [6].

ANSICHT: Die Ansicht eines Weisen und den Rat eines Greisen soll man nicht von sich weisen [53].

ARBEIT: Wie die Arbeit, so der Lohn [3].

ARM: Besser arm in Ehren als reich in Schanden [10].

ARZT: Arzt, hilf Dir selbst [94].

AUFSTEHEN: Legst Du Dich mit den Hunden, so stehst Du mit den Flöhen auf [44].

AUGE: Die Augen sind oft größer als der Magen [23]; Vier Augen sehen mehr als zwei [28]; Aus den Augen, aus dem Sinn [91]; Was die Augen sehen, glaubt das Herz [101].

BÄR: Man darf niemals die Haut eines Bären verkaufen, bevor man ihn erlegt hat [54].

BART: Sie streiten um des Kaisers Bart [57].

BAUM: Alte Bäume soll man nicht verpflanzen [98].

BEGINNEN: Vorm Beginnen sich besinnen, macht gewinnen [63]; Frisch begonnen, ist halb gewonnen [119].

BEHARRLICHKEIT: Beharrlichkeit führt zum Ziel [93].

BESEN: Neue Besen kehren gut [76].

BESINNEN (sich): Vorm Beginnen sich besinnen, macht gewinnen [63].

BESORGEN: Was Du heute kannst besorgen, das verschiebe nicht auf morgen [73].

BESSER: Besser allein als in schlechter Gesellschaft [7]; Besser ein kleiner Fisch als gar nichts auf dem Tisch [9]; Besser arm in Ehren als reich in Schanden [10]; Vorbeugen ist besser als heilen [96]; Heiraten ist gut, ledig bleiben ist besser [125].

BESTE: Hunger ist der beste Koch [51].

EILE: Eile mit Weile [71].

EINIGKEIT: Einigkeit macht stark [116].

EMPFEHLEN (sich): Er hat sich französisch empfohlen [42].

ENDE: Ende gut, alles gut [2].

ENTSCHULDIGEN (sich): Wer sich entschuldigt, klagt sich an [46].

ERNTEN: Die einen säen, und die anderen ernten [87].

ERLEGEN: Man darf niemals die Haut eines Bären verkaufen, bevor man ihn erlegt hat [54].

ESEL: Ein Weib, ein Esel und eine Nuß, diese drei man klopfen muß [128].

ESSEN: Man lebt nicht, um zu essen, man ißt, um zu leben [62].

ETWAS: Wer etwas will, muß vieles fordern [5].

FALLEN: Wo gehobelt wird, fallen Späne [84].

FAUL: Die Faulen und die Dreisten schreien am meisten [126].

FEHLER: Aus Fehlern lernt man [67].

FENSTER: Wenn die Not an die Türe klopft, springt die Liebe aus dem Fenster [122].

FEUER: Feuer und Wasser sind zwei gute Diener, aber zwei schlimme Herren [25].

BETTEN (sich): Wie man sich bettet, so liegt man [4].

BEWAFFNET: Er ist bis an die Zähne bewaffnet [37].

BILDEN: Reisen bildet [48].

BLIND: Blinder Eifer schadet nur [34]; Keiner ist so blind wie derjenige, der nicht sehen will [80].

BLUT: Gewohnheiten gehen in Fleisch und Blut über. [33].

BRATEN: Ungefangene Fische kann man nicht braten [72].

BREI: Viele Köche verderben den Brei [115].

BRINGEN: Wer bringt, ist überall willkommen [114].

DACH: Lieber den Spatz in der Hand als die Taube auf dem Dach [8].

DIEB: Gelegenheit macht Diebe [89].

DIENER: Feuer und Wasser sind sind zwei gute Diener, aber zwei schlimme Herren [25].

DORN: Keine Rose ohne Dornen [79].

DREI: Ein Weib, ein Esel und eine Nuß, diese drei man klopfen muß [128].

DREIST: Die Faulen und die Dreisten schreien am meisten [126].

EHRE: Besser arm in Ehren als reich in Schanden [10].

EHRLICH: Ehrlich währt am längsten [49].

EIFER: Blinder Eifer schadet nur [34].

FINDEN: Wer sucht, der findet [47].

FISCH: Besser ein kleiner Fisch als gar nichts auf dem Tisch [9]; Ungefangene Fische kann man nicht braten [72].

FLEISCH: Gewohnheiten gehen in Fleisch und Blut über [33].

FLEISS: Ohne Bleiß kein Preis [104].

FLOH: Er hat mir einen Floh ins Ohr gesetzt [41]; Legst Du Dich mit den Hunden, so stehst Du mit den Flöhen auf [44].

FORDERN: Wer etwas will, muß vieles fordern [5].

FRANZÖSISCH: Er hat sich französisch empfohlen [42].

FRAU: Wie die Frau, so die Magd [61].

FREIEN: Für Geld gefreit, ein goldnes Joch [45].

FREUND: Ein Narr und sein Geld sind nicht lange Freund in der Welt [27].

FRIEDE: Wer Frieden haben will, muß zum Krieg rüsten [52].

FRISCH: Frisch begonnen, ist halb gewonnen [119].

FÜHREN: Er führt mich an der Nase herum [39]; Beharrlichkeit führt zum Ziel [93].

FÜRSORGE: Übertriebene Fürsorge schadet nur [16].

FUSS: Er steht mit einem Fuß im Grab [38].

GEBEN: Geben ist seliger denn nehmen [56].

GEDULD: Auch Geduld hat Grenzen [111].

GEFÄLLIGKEIT: Eine Gefälligkeit ist der andern wert [85].

GEHEN: Nicht nur Heilige gehen zur Kirche [1].

GELD: Ein Narr und sein Geld sind nicht lange Freund in der Welt [27]; Für Geld gefreit, ein goldnes Joch [45]; Geld kommt zu Geld [68]; Geld ist die Wurzel allen Übels [69]; Geld regiert die Welt [70].

GELEGENHEIT: Gelegenheit macht Diebe [89].

GERN: Gleich und gleich gesellt sich gern [12].

GESCHÄFT: Geschäft ist Geschäft [13].

GESCHMACK: Über Geschmack läßt sich nicht streiten [108].

GESELLEN (sich): Gleich und gleich gesellt sich gern [12].

GESELLSCHAFT: Besser allein als in schlechter Gesellschaft [7].

GESUNDHEIT: Gesundheit ist das höchste Gut [35].

GEWINNEN: Vorm Beginnen sich besinnen, macht gewinnen [63]; Frisch begonnen, ist halb gewonnen [119].

GEWOHNHEIT: Gewohnheiten gehen in Fleisch und Blut über [33].

GLAUBEN: Was die Augen sehen, glaubt das Herz [101].

GLEICH: Gleich und gleich gesellt sich gern [12].

GLÜCKLICH: Keiner ist vor seinem Tod glücklich zu preisen [15].

GOLD: Reden ist Silber, Schweigen ist Gold [105].

GOTT: Gott schuf die Natur, die Städte sind vom Menschen [30].

GRAB: Er steht mit einem Fuß im Grab [38].

GREIFEN: Einem nackten Mann kann man nicht in die Tasche greifen [74].

GREIS: Die Ansicht eines Weisen und den Rat eines Greisen soll man nicht von sich weisen [53].

GRENZE: Auch Geduld hat Grenzen [111].

GROSS: Die Augen sind oft größer als der Magen [23].

GUT (adj): Ende gut, alles gut [2]; Feuer und Wasser sind zwei gute Diener, aber zwei schlimme Herren [25]; Neue Besen kehren gut [76]; Guter Rat kommt über Nacht [77]; Keine Nachricht, gute Nachricht [78]; Heiraten ist gut, ledig bleiben ist besser [125].

GUT (subst.): Gesundheit ist das höchste Gut [35].

HALB: Frisch begonnen, ist halb gewonnen [119].

HAND: Kalte Hände, warmes Herz [20].

HAUS: Wohltun beginnt zu Hause [18]; Man sieht am Hause, wes Sinnes der Herr ist [50]; Wenn die Katze aus dem Haus ist, tanzen die Mäuse auf dem Tisch [123].

HAUT: Man darf niemals die Haut eines Bären verkaufen, bevor man ihn erlegt hat [54].

HEILEN: Vorbeugen ist besser als heilen [96].

HEILIGER: Nicht nur Heilige gehen zur Kirche [1].

HEIRATEN: Heiraten ist gut, ledig bleiben ist besser [125].

HEISS: Das Eisen muß man schmieden, solange es heiß ist [106].

HELFEN (sich): Arzt, hilf Dir selbst [94]; Hilfst Du mir, so helf ich Dir [99].

HERR: Feuer und Wasser sind zwei gute Diener, aber zwei schlimme Herren [25]; Man sieht am Hause, wes Sinnes der Herr ist [50].

HERZ: Kalte Hände, warmes Herz [20]; Was die Augen sehen, glaubt das Herz [101].

HEUEN: Im Regen ist schlecht heuen [66].

HEUTE: Was Du heute kannst besorgen, das verschiebe nicht auf morgen [73].

HINKEN: Jeder Vergleich hinkt [21].

HOBELN: Wo gehobelt wird, fallen Späne [84].

HÖCHST: Gesundheit ist das höchste Gut [35].

HÖREN: Keiner ist so taub wie derjenige, der nicht hören will [81].

HUND: Legst Du Dich mit den Hunden, so stehst Du mit den Flöhen auf [44]; Schlafende Hunde soll man nicht wecken [58].

HUNGER: Hunger ist der beste Koch [51].

INNER: Auf die inneren Werte kommt es an [6].

JEDER: Jeder Vergleich hinkt [21]; Jeder Krämer lobt seine Ware [22]; Jeder soll vor seiner eigenen Türe kehren [107].

JOCH: Für Geld gefreit, ein goldnes Joch [45].

JUNG: Wie die Alten sungen, so zwitschern auch die Jungen [19].

KAISER: Sie streiten um des Kaisers Bart [57].

KALT: Kalte Hände, warmes Herz [20].

KATZE: Wenn die Katze aus dem Haus ist, tanzen die Mäuse auf dem Tisch [123].

KAUFEN: Wer Unnötiges kauft, muß bald Notwendiges verkaufen [43].

KEHREN: Neue Besen kehren gut [76]; Jeder soll vor seiner eigenen Türe kehren [107].

KEIN: Keiner ist vor seinem Tod glücklich zu preisen [15]; Keine Nachricht, gute Nachrich [78]; Keine Rose ohne Dornen [79]; Keiner ist so blind wie derjenige, der nicht sehen will [80]; Keiner ist so taub wie derjenige, der nicht hören will [81].

KIND: Die Alten werden zweimal Kinder [83].

KIRCHE: Nicht nur Heilige gehen zur Kirche [1].

KIRSCHE: Wer die Kirschen will, muß auch die Steine nehmen [64].

KLEIDER: Kleider machen Leute [29].

KLEIN: Besser ein kleiner Fisch als gar nichts auf dem Tisch [9].

KLOPFEN: Wenn die Not an die Türe klopft, springt die Liebe aus dem Fenster [122]; Ein Weib, ein Esel und eine Nuß, diese drei man klopfen muß [128].

KOCH: Hunger ist der beste Koch [51]; Viele Köche verderben den Brei [115].

KOMMEN: Wer zuerst kommt, mahlt zuerst [26]; Geld kommt zu Geld [68]; Guter Rat kommt über Nacht [77]; Rat nach der Tat kommt zu spät [120].

KÖNIG: Auch ein König ist nur ein Mensch [17].

KOPF: Die Schulden wachsen ihm über den Kopf [92].

KRÄMER: Jeder Krämer lobt seine Ware [22].

KRIEG: Wer Frieden haben will, muß zum Krieg rüsten [52].

KUNST: Die Kunst ist lang, und kurz ist unser Leben [59].

KURZ: Die Kunst ist lang, und kurz ist unser Leben [59].

LAND: Andere Länder, andere Sitten [121].

LANG: Die Kunst ist lang, und kurz ist unser Leben [59].

LÄNGST: Ehrlich währt am längsten [49].

LASTER: Müßiggang ist aller Laster Anfang [14].

LEBEN: Die Kunst ist lang, und kurz ist unser Leben [59]; Man lebt nicht, um zu essen, man ißt, um zu leben [62].

LEDIG: Heiraten ist gut, ledig bleiben ist besser [125].

LEGEN (sich): Legst Du Dich mit den Hunden, so stehst Du mit den Flöhen auf [44].

LERNEN: Aus Fehlern lernt man [67]; Man ist nie zu alt zum Lernen [75].

LEUTE: Kleider machen Leute [29].

LIEBE: Alte Liebe rostet nicht [82]; Wenn die Not an die Türe klopft, springt die Liebe aus dem Fenster [122].

LIEBEN: Liebe Deinen Nachbarn, aber reiß den Zaun nicht ein [65].

LIEBER: Lieber den Spatz in der Hand als die Taube auf dem Dach [8]; Lieber spät als nie [11].

LIEGEN: Wie man sich bettet, so liegt man [4]; In der Abwechslung liegt das Vergnügen [32].

LOBEN: Jeder Krämer lobt seine Ware [22].

LOHN: Wie die Arbeit, so der Lohn [3].

MACHEN: Kleider machen Leute [29]; Eine Schwalbe macht noch keinen Sommer [88]; Gelegenheit macht Diebe [89]; Einigkeit macht stark [116].

MAGD: Wie die Frau, so die Magd [61].

MAGEN: Die Augen sind oft größer als der Magen [23].

MAHLEN: Wer zuerst kommt, mahlt zuerst [26].

MANN: Einem nackten Mann kann man nicht in die Tasche greifen [74].

MAUS: Wenn die Katze aus dem Haus ist, tanzen die Mäuse auf dem Tisch [123].

MEIST: Die Faulen und die Dreisten schreien am meisten [126].

MENSCH: Auch ein König ist nur ein Mensch [17]; Gott schuf die Natur, die Städte sind vom Menschen [30]; Man muß die Menschen nehmen, wie sie sind [118].

MORGEN: Was Du heute kannst besorgen, das verschiebe nicht auf morgen [73].

MÜSSIGGANG: Müßiggang ist aller Laster Anfang [14].

MUTTER: Wie der Vater, so der Sohn; wie die Mutter, so die Tochter [60].

NACHBAR: Liebe Deinen Nachbarn, aber reiß den Zaun nicht ein [65].

NACHRICHT: Keine Nachricht, gute Nachricht [78].

NACHT: Guter Rat kommt über Nacht [77].

NACKT: Einem nackten Mann kann man nicht in die Tasche greifen [74].

NADEL: Er sitzt wie auf Nadeln [40].

NARR: Ein Narr und sein Geld sind nicht lange Freund in der Welt [27].

NASE: Er führt mich an der Nase herum [39].

NATUR: Gott schuf die Natur, die Städte sind vom Menschen [30].

NEHMEN: Geben ist seliger denn nehmen [56]; Man muß die Menschen nehmen, wie sie sind [118].

NEU: Neue Besen kehren gut [76].

NICHTS: Besser ein kleiner Fisch als gar nichts auf dem Tisch [9].

NIE (-mals): Lieber spät als nie [11]; Man darf niemals die Haut eines Bären verkaufen, bevor man ihn erlegt hat [54]; Man ist nie zu alt zum Lernen [75].

NOT: Wenn die Not an die Türe klopft, springt die Liebe aus dem Fenster [122].

NOTWENDIG: Wer Unnötiges kauft, muß bald Notwendiges verkaufen [43].

NUSS: Ein Weib, ein Esel und eine Nuß, diese drei man klopfen muß [128].

ÖFFENTLICHKEIT: Man soll schmutzige Wäsche nicht in der Öffentlichkeit waschen [86].

OHR: Er hat mir einen Floh ins Ohr gesetzt [41];Wände haben Ohren [117].

PFERD: Ein williges Pferd soll man nicht spornen [31].

PREIS: Ohne Fleiß kein Preis [104].

PREISEN: Keiner ist vor seinem Tod glücklich zu preisen [15].

RAT: Die Ansicht eines Weisen und den Rat eines Greisen soll man nicht von sich weisen [53]; Guter Rat kommt über Nacht [77]; Rat nach der Tat kommt zu spät [120].

RATTE: Die Ratten verlassen das sinkende Schiff [97].

REDEN: Reden ist Silber, Schweigen ist Gold [105]; Reden hat seine Zeit, und Schweigen hat seine Zeit [113].

REGEN: Im Regen ist schlecht heuen [66].

REGIEREN: Geld regiert die Welt [70].

REICH: Besser arm in Ehren als reich in Schanden [10].

REISEN: Reisen bildet [48].

RESPEKT: Vertraulichkeit schadet dem Respekt [24].

ROSE: Keine Rose ohne Dornen [79].

ROSTEN: Alte Liebe rostet nicht [82].

RÜSTEN: Wer Frieden haben will, muß zum Krieg rüsten [52].

SÄEN: Die einen säen, und die anderen ernten [87].

SAFT: Er soll in seinem eigenen Saft schmoren [36].

SAGEN: Sage mir, mit wem Du umgehst, und ich sage Dir, wer Du bist [109].

SCHADEN: Übertriebene Fürsorge schadet nur [16]; Vertraulichkeit schadet dem Respekt [24]; Blinder Eifer schadet nur [34].

SCHAF: Überall gibt es schwarze Schafe [110].

SCHAFFEN: Gott schuf die Natur, die Städte sind vom Menschen [30].

SCHAFSPELZ: Ein Wolf im Schafspelz [127].

SCHANDE: Besser arm in Ehren als reich in Schanden [10].

SCHIFF: Die Ratten verlassen das sinkende Schiff [97].

SCHLAFEN: Schlafende Hunde soll man nicht wecken [58].

SCHLECHT: Besser allein als in schlechter Gesellschaft [7]; In Regen ist schlecht heuen [66]; Der Schuster trägt die schlechtesten Schuhe [102].

SCHLIMM: Feuer und Wasser sind zwei gute Diener, aber zwei schlimme Herren [25].

SCHMIEDEN: Das Eisen muß man schmieden, solange es heiß ist [106].

SCHMOREN: Er soll in seinem eigenen Saft schmoren [36].

SCHMUTZIG: Man soll schmutzige Wäsche nicht in der Öffentlichkeit waschen [86].

SCHON: Alles ist schon einmal da gewesen [112].

SCHREIEN: Die Faulen und die Dreisten schreien am meisten [126].

SCHUH: Der Schuster trägt die schlechtesten Schuhe [102].

SCHULDEN: Die Schulden wachsen ihm über den Kopf [92].

SCHUSTER: Der Schuster trägt die schlechtesten Schuhe [102].

SCHWALBE: Eine Schwalbe macht noch keine Sommer [88].

SCHWARZ: Überall gibt es schwarze Schafe [110].

SCHWEIGEN: Wer schweigt, stimmt zu [103]; Reden ist Silber, Schweigen ist Gold [105]; Reden hat seine Zeit, und Schweigen hat seine Zeit [113].

SEHEN: Vier Augen sehen mehr als zwei [28]; Man sieht am Hause, wes Sinnes der Herr ist [50]; Keiner ist so blind wie derjenige, der nicht sehen will [80]; Was die Augen sehen, glaubt das Herz [101].

SELBST: Arzt, hilf Dir selbst [94].

SELIG: Geben ist seliger denn nehmen [56].

SETZEN: Er hat mir einen Floh ins Ohr gesetzt [41].

SILBER: Reden ist Silber, Schweigen ist Gold [105].

SINGEN: Wie die Alten sungen, so zwitschern auch die Jungen [19].

SINN: Man sieht am Hause, wes Sinnes der Herr ist [50]; Aus den Augen, aus dem Sinn [91].

SITTE: Andere Zeiten, andere Sitten [90]; Andere Länder, andere Sitten [121].

SITZEN: Er sitzt wie auf Nadeln [40].

SOHN: Wie der Vater, so der Sohn; wie die Mutter, so die Tochter [60].

SOMMER: Eine Schwalbe macht noch keinen Sommer [88].

SPAN: Wo gehobelt wird, fallen Späne [84].

SPÄT: Lieber spät als nie [11]; Rat nach der Tat kommt zu spät [120].

SPATZ: Lieber den Spatz in der Hand als die Taube auf dem Dach [8].

SPORNEN: Ein williges Pferd soll man nicht spornen [31].

SPRINGEN: Wenn die Not an die Türe klopft, springt die Liebe aus dem Fenster [i22].

STADT: Gott schuf die Natur, die Städte sind vom Menschen [30].

STARK: Einigkeit macht stark [116].

STEHEN: Er steht mit einem Fuß im Grab [38].

STEIN: Wer die Kirschen will, muß auch die Steine nehmen [64].

STREITEN (sich): Sie streiten um des Kaisers Bart [57]; Über Geschmack läßt sich nicht streiten [108].

SUCHEN: Wer sucht, der findet [47].

TANZEN: Wenn die Katze aus dem Haus ist, tanzen die Mäuse auf dem Tisch [123].

TASCHE: Einem nackten Mann kann man nicht in die Tasche greifen [74].

TAT: Rat nach der Tat kommt zu spät [120].

TAUB: Keiner ist so taub wie derjenige, der nicht hören will [81].

TAUBE: Lieber den Spatz in der Hand als die Taube auf dem Dach [8].

TISCH: Besser ein kleiner Fisch als gar nichts auf dem Tisch [9]; Wenn die Katze aus dem Haus ist, tanzen die Mäuse auf dem Tisch [123].

TOCHTER: Wie der Vater, so der Sohn; wie die Mutter, so die Tochter [60].

TOD: Keiner ist vor seinem Tod glücklich zu preisen [15].

TRAGEN: Der Schuster trägt die schlechtesten Schuhe [102].

TÜRE: Jeder soll vor seiner eigenen Türe kehren [107]; Wenn die Not an die Türe klopft, springt die Liebe aus dem Fenster [122].

ÜBEL: Geld ist die Wurzel allen Übels [69].

ÜBERALL: Überall gibt es schwarze Schafe [110]; Wer bringt, ist überall willkommen [114].

ÜBERTRIEBEN: Übertriebene Fürsorge schadet nur [16].

ÜBUNG: Übung macht den Meister [95].

UMGEHEN: Sage mir, mit wem Du umgehst, und ich sage Dir, wer Du bist [109].

UNGEFANGEN: Ungefangene Fische kann man nicht braten [72].

UNNÖTIG: Wer Unnötiges kauft, muß bald Notwendiges verkaufen [43].

VATER: Wie der Vater, so der Sohn; wie die Mutter, so die Tochter [60].

VERDERBEN: Viele Köche verderben den Brei [115].

VERGLEICH: Jeder Vergleich hinkt [21].

VERGNÜGEN: In der Abwechslung liegt das Vergnügen [32].

VERKAUFEN: Wer Unnötiges kauft, muß bald Notwendiges verkaufen [43]; Man darf niemals die Haut eines Bären verkaufen, bevor man ihn erlegt hat [54].

VERLASSEN: Die Ratten verlassen das sinkende Schiff [97].

VERPFLANZEN: Alte Bäume soll man nicht verpflanzen [98].

VERSCHIEBEN: Was Du heute kannst besorgen, das verschiebe nicht auf morgen [73].

VERTRAULICHKEIT: Vertraulichkeit schadet dem Respekt [24].

VIEL: Wer etwas will, muß vieles fordern [5]; Viele Köche verderben den Brei [115].

VIER: Vier Augen sehen mehr als zwei [28].

VORBEUGEN: Vorbeugen ist besser als heilen [96].

WACHSEN: Die Schulden wachsen ihm über den Kopf [92].

WAGEN: Erst wägen, dann wagen [100].

WÄGEN: Erst wägen, dann wagen [100].

WÄHREN: Ehrlich währt am längsten [49].

WAHRHEIT: Im Wein ist Wahrheit [55].

WAND: Wände haben Ohren [117].

WARE: Jeder Krämer lobt seine Ware [22].

WARM: Kalte Hände, warmes Herz [20].

WÄSCHE: Man soll schmutzige Wäsche nicht in der Öffentlichkeit waschen [86].

WASSER: Feuer und Wasser sind zwei gute Diener, aber zwei schlimme Herren [25].

WECKEN: Schlafende Hunde soll man nicht wecken [58].

WEG: Wo ein Wille ist, ist auch ein Weg [124].

WEIB: Ein Weib, ein Esel und eine Nuß, diese drei man klopfen muß [128].

WEILE: Eile mit Weile [71].

WEIN: Im Wein ist Wahrheit [55].

WEISE: Die Ansicht eines Weisen und den Rat eines Greisen soll man nicht von sich weisen [53].

WEISEN (von sich): Die Ansicht eines Weisen und den Rat eines Greisen soll man nicht von sich weisen [53].

WELT: Ein Narr und sein Geld sind nicht lange Freund in der Welt [27]; Geld regiert die Welt [70].

WERT (adj.): Eine Gefälligkeit ist der andern wert [85].

WERT (subst.): Auf die inneren Werte kommt es an [6].

WILLE: Wo ein Wille ist, ist auch ein Weg [124].

WILLIG: Ein williges Pferd soll man nicht spornen [31].

WILLKOMMEN: Wer bringt, ist überall willkommen [114].

WOHLTUN: Wohltun beginnt zu Hause [18].

WOLF: Ein Wolf im Schafspelz [127].

WOLLEN: Wer etwas will, muß vieles fordern [5]; Keiner ist so blind wie derjenige, der nicht sehen will [80]; Keiner ist so taub wie derjenige, der nicht hören will [81].

WURZEL: Geld ist die Wurzel allen Übels [69].

ZAHN: Er ist bis an die Zähne bewaffnet [37].

ZAUN: Liebe Deinen Nachbarn, aber reiß den Zaun nicht ein [65].

ZEIT: Andere Zeiten, andere Sitten [90]; Reden hat seine Zeit, und Schweigen hat seine Zeit [113].

ZIEL: Beharrlichkeit führt zum Ziel [93].

ZUERST: Wer zuerst kommt, mahlt zuerst [26].

ZUSTIMMEN: Wer schweigt, stimmt zu [103].

ZWEI (-mal): Feuer und Wasser sind zwei gute Diener, aber zwei schlimme Herren [25]; Vier Augen sehen mehr als zwei [28]; Die Alten werden zweimal Kinder [83].

ZWITSCHERN: Wie die Alten sungen, so zwitschern auch die Jungen [19].

ABANDONAR: Las ratas abandonan el barco que se hunde [97].

ABRIR: El dinero abre todas las puertas [70].

ACABAR: Bien está lo que bien acaba [2]; Nadie se alabe hasta que acabe [15]; Quien bien empieza, bien acaba [119].

ACERTAR: El errar es maestro del acertar [67].

ACOMPAÑADO: Mejor solo que mal acompañado [7].

ACOSTAR (se): Quien con perros se acuesta, con pulgas se levanta [44].

ACUSAR: Quien se excusa, se acusa [46].

AGARRAR: Me tiene agarrado por las narices [39].

AGUA: El fuego y el agua son buenos servidores pero ruines amos [25].

ALABAR: Nadie se alabe hasta que acabe [15]; Cada ollero su olla alaba [22].

ALCANZAR: Con la paciencia todo se alcanza [93].

AMAR: Ama tu vecino pero no deshagas tu seto [65].

AMO: El fuego y el agua son buenos servidores pero ruines amos [25].

AMOR: El primer amor es el último en olvidarse [82]; Cuando el hambre entra por la puerta, el amor huye por la ventana [122].

ANDAR: Dime con quien andas y te diré quien eres [109].

APRENDER: Nunca es tarde para aprender [75].

APRESURAR: Quien se apura, su muerte apresura [16].

APRISA: Cosa hecha aprisa, cosa de risa [34].

APURAR (se): Quien se apura, su muerte apresura [16].

ARBOL: Mientras hace calor se pelan los árboles [66].

ARMADO: Está armado hasta los dientes [37].

ARTE: El arte es largo y la vida breve [59].

ASNO: El asno y la mujer, a palos se han de vencer [128].

ASTILLA: De tal palo, tal astilla [60].

AVARICIA: La avaricia es la raíz de todos los males [69].

BAILAR: Cuando el gato no está, los ratones bailan [123].

BARCO: Más vale honra sin barcos, que barcos sin honra [10]; Las ratas abandonan el barco que se hunde [97].

BARRER: Escoba nueva barre bien [76].

BASURA: Hermosura, al fin basura [6].

BATIR: Al hierro caliente, batir de repente [106].

BIEN: Bien está lo que bien acaba [2]; La caridad bien entendida empieza por uno mismo [18]; Escoba nueva barre bien [76]; Quien bien empieza, bien acaba [119]; El que se casa hace bien, y el que no se casa hace mejor [125].

BIENAVENTURADA: Más bienaventurada cosa es dar que recibir [56].

BOCA: A la vulpeja dormida no le cae nada en la boca [104].

BREVE: El arte es largo y la vida breve [59].

BUENO: A falta de pan buenas son tortas [9]; El fuego y el agua son buenos servidores pero ruines amos [25]; A buen hambre no hay pan duro [51]; No es bueno pelear por un hueso [57]; Ninguna nueva, buenas nuevas [78].

BUSCAR: Quien busca, halla [47]; No hay que buscar tres pies al gato [58].

CABALLO: Caballo que vuela, no quiere espuelas [31].

CADA (cual): Cada cual en su casa y Dios en la de todos [107].

CAER: A la vulpeja dormida no le cae nada en la boca [104].

CALIENTE: Manos frías, corazón caliente [20]; Al hierro caliente, batir de repente [106].

CALOR: Mientras hace calor se pelan los árboles [66].

CALLAR: Quien calla, otorga [103]; Hay un tiempo para hablar y un tiempo para callar [113].

CAMA: Quien mala cama hace, en ella yace [4].

CAMPO: Dios hizo el campo y el hombre la ciudad [30].

CAN: Quien quiere a Beltrán, quiere a su can [64].

CAPITAL: La honradez es el mejor capital [49].

CARIDAD: La caridad bien entendida empieza por uno mismo [18].

CASA: En casa de mujer rica, ella manda y ella grita [45]; Por la casa se conoce al dueño [50]; Los trapos sucios se lavan en casa [86]; En casa del herrero, cuchara de palo [102]; Cada cual en su casa y Dios en la de todos [107].

CASAR (se): El que se casa hace bien, y el que no se casa hace mejor [125].

CAUSA: La familiaridad es causa de menosprecio [24].

CAUTIVAR: Los dones cautivan hasta a los dioses [114].

CAZAR: Me reparto la piel del oso antes de cazarlo [54].

CIEGO: No hay peor ciego que el que no quiere ver [80].

CIUDAD: Dios hizo el campo y el hombre la ciudad [30].

COCER (se): Se cuece en su propia salsa [36].

COMER: No hay que vivir para comer, sino comer para vivir [62].

COMPARACION: Toda comparación es odiosa [21].

COMPONEDOR: Muchos componedores descomponen la novia (115).

COMPRAR: Quien compra lo que no puede, vende lo que le duele [43].

CONOCER: Por la casa se conoce al dueño [50].

CONSEJO: Consejo, tómalo del hombre viejo [53]; La noche trae consejo [77]; Hecho el hecho, huelga el consejo [120].

CORAZON: Manos frías, corazón caliente [20]; Ojos que no ven, corazón que no siente [91].

COSA: Cosa hecha aprisa, cosa de risa [34]; Más bienaventurada cosa es dar que recibir [56]; Tomemos las cosas como vienen [118].

COSECHA: Hay quien siembra y quien cosecha [87].

COSTUMBRE: La costumbre es otra naturaleza [33]; A otros tiempos, otras costumbres [90].

CRECER: Viejas plantas traspuestas, ni crecen ni medran [98].

CREER: Ver es creer [101].

CRIADA: A tal dama, tal criada [61].

CUATRO: Cuatro ojos ven más que dos [28].

CUCHARA: En casa del herrero, cuchara de palo [102].

CURAR: Médico, cúrate a ti mismo [94]; Más vale prevenir que curar [96].

DAMA: A tal dama, tal criada [61].

DAR: Pide lo más y algo te darán [5]; Más bienaventurada cosa es dar que recibir [56].

DEBER: Deber a todo el mundo [92].

DECIR: Lo que el niño oyó en el hogar, eso dice en el portal [19]; Dime con quien andas y te diré quien eres [109]; No hay nada que no esté ya dicho [112].

DEJAR: No dejes para mañana lo que puedes hacer hoy [73].

DESCARRIADA: En cada rebaño hay una oveja descarriada [110].

DESCOMPONER: Muchos componedores descomponen la novia [115].

DESHACER: Ama tu vecino pero no deshagas tu seto [65].

DESNUDO: Desnudo nací, desnudo me hallo, ni pierdo ni gano [74].

DESPACIO: Vísteme despacio, que tengo prisa [71].

DESPEDIR (se): Se despide a la francesa [42].

DIA: La vejez tornó por los días en que nació [83].

DIENTE: Está armado hasta los dientes [37].

DINERO: El tonto y su dinero son pronto separados [27]; Primero es la salud que el dinero [35]; Dinero llama a dinero [68]; El dinero abre todas las puertas [70].

DIOS: Dios hizo el campo y el hombre la ciudad [30]; Cada cual en su casa y Dios en la de todos [107].

DIOSES: Los dones cautivan hasta a los dioses [114].

DOLER: Quien compra lo que no puede, vende lo que le duele [43].

DON: Los dones cautivan hasta a los dioses [114].

DORMIDA: A la vulpeja dormida no le cae nada en la boca [104].

DUEÑO: Por la casa se conoce al dueño [50].

DURO: A buen hambre no hay pan duro [51].

ECHAR: Me ha echado la pulga detrás de la oreja [41].

EJERCICIO: El ejercicio hace maestro [95].

EMPEZAR: La caridad bien entendida empieza por uno mismo [18]; Quien bien empieza, bien acaba [119].

ENCERRADO: No le llames grano hasta que no esté encerrado [72].

ENTENDIDA: La caridad bien entendida empieza por uno mismo [18].

ENTRAR: Cuando el hambre entra por la puerta, el amor huye por la ventana [122].

ERRAR: El errar es maestro del acertar [67].

ESCOBA: Escoba nueva barre bien [76].

ESCRITO: Sobre gustos no hay nada escrito [108].

ESPINA: Está sobre espinas [40]; No hay rosa sin espinas [79].

ESPUELA: Caballo que vuela, no quiere espuelas [31].

ESTUDIAR: No todos los que estudian son letrados [1].

EXCUSAR (se): Quien se excusa, se acusa [46].

FALTA: A falta de pan buenas son tortas [9].

FAMILIARIDAD: La familiaridad es causa de menosprecio [24].

FAVOR: Un favor se paga con otro [85].

FRANCESA: Se despide a la francesa [42].

FRIA: Manos frías, corazón caliente [20].

FUEGO: El fuego y el agua son buenos servidores pero ruines amos [25].

FUERZA: La unión hace la fuerza [116].

GANAR: Desnudo nací, desnudo me hallo, ni pierdo ni gano [74].

GATO: No hay que buscar tres pies al gato [58];

Cuando el gato no está, los ratones bailan [123].

GENTE: Viajando se instruye la gente [48].

GOLONDRINA: Una golondrina no hace verano [88].

GRANO: No le llames grano hasta que no esté encerrado [72].

GRITAR: En casa de mujer rica, ella manda y ella grita [45].

GUERRA: Si quieres la paz, prepárate para la guerra [52].

GUSTO: En la variedad está el gusto [32]; Sobre gustos no hay nada escrito [108].

HABITO: El hábito hace al monje [29].

HABLAR: Hay un tiempo para hablar y un tiempo para callar [113].

HACER: Quien mala cama hace, en ella yace [4]; No dejes para mañana le que puedes hacer hoy [73]; No se hacen tortillas sin huevos [84]; Una golondrina no hace verano [88];

La ocasión hace al ladrón [89]; El ejercicio hace maestro [95]; La unión hace la fuerza [116]; Hecho el hecho, huelga el consejo [120]; Cuando a Roma fueres, haz come vieres [121].

HALLAR: Quien busca, halla [47]; Desnudo nací, desnudo me hallo, ni pierdo ni gano [74].

HAMBRE: A buen hambre no hay pan duro [51]; Cuando el hambre entra por la puerta, el amor huye por la ventana [122].

HASTA: Nadie se alabe hasta que acabe [15]; Está armado hasta los dientes [37]; No le llames grano hasta que esté encerrado [72]; Los dones cautivan hasta a los dioses [114].

HERMOSURA: Hermosura, al fin basura [6].

HERRERO: En casa del herrero, cuchara de palo [102].

HIERRO: Al hierro caliente, batir de repente [106].

HOGAR: Lo que el niño oyó en el hogar, eso dice en el portal [19].

HOMBRE: Dios hizo el campo y el hombre la ciudad [30].

HONRA: Más vale honra sin barcos, que barcos sin honra [10].

HONRADEZ: La honradez es el mejor capital [49].

HOY: Mejor es huevo hoy que pollo mañana [8];

No dejes para mañana lo que puedes hacer hoy [73];
Hoy por ti, mañana por mi [99].

HUELGA: Hecho el hecho, huelga el consejo [120].

HUESO: No es bueno pelear por un hueso [57].

HUEVO: Mejor es huevo hoy que pollo mañana [8].
No se hacen tortillas sin huevos [84].

HUIR: Cuando el hambre entra por la puerta, el amor huye
por la ventata [122].

HUNDIR: Las ratas abandonan el barco que se hunde [97].

INSTRUIR (se): Viajando se instruye la gente [48].
IR: Cuando a Roma fueres, haz como vieres [121].

LADRADOR: Perro ladrador, poco mordedor [126].

LADRON: la ocasión hace al ladrón [89].

LARGO: El arte es largo y la vida breve [59].

LAVAR: Los trapos sucios se lavan en casa [86].

LETRADO: No todos los que estudian son letrados [1].

LEVANTAR (se): Quien con perros se acuesta, con pulgas se
levanta [44].

LIMITE: La paciencia tiene un límite [111].

LOBO: Un lobo con piel de oveja [127].

LLAMAR: Dinero llama a dinero [68]; No le llames grano
hasta que esté encerrado [72].

LLENAR: Se llena antes el papo que el ojo [23].

MAESTRO: El errar es maestro del acertar [67];
El ejercicio hace maestro [95].

MAL (adverbio): Mejor solo que mal acompañado [7].

MALE (sustantivo): Muchos males engendra la ociosidad [14];
La avaricia es la raíz de todos los males [69].

MANDAR: En casa de mujer rica, ella manda y ella grita [45].

MANO: Manos frías, corazón caliente [20].

MAÑANA: Mejor es huevo hoy que pollo mañana [8];
No dejes para mañana lo que puedes hacer hoy [73];
Hoy por ti, mañana por mi [99].

MAS VALE: Más vale honra sin barcos que barcos sin honra [10]; Más vale tarde que nunca [11]; Más vale prevenir que curar [96].

MEDICO: Médico, cúrate a ti mismo [94].

MEDRAR: Viejas plantas traspuestas, ni crecen ni medran [98].

MEJOR: Los segundos pensamientos son los mejores [100].

MENOSPRECIO: La familiaridad es causa de menosprecio [24].

MIRAR: El perro puede mirar al rey [17]; Mirar antes de saltar [63].

MONJE: El hábito hace al monje [29].

MORDEDOR: Perro ladrador, poco mordedor [126].

MUCHOS: Muchos componedores descomponen la novia [115].

MUERTE: Quien se apura, su muerte apresura [16].

MUJER: En casa de mujer rica, ella manda y ella grita [45]; El asno y la mujer, a palos se han de vencer [128].

MUNDO: Deber a todo el mundo [92].

NACER: Desnudo nací, desnudo me hallo, ni pierdo ni gano [74]; La vejez tornó por los días en que nació [83].

NADA: A la vulpeja dormida no le cae nada en la boca [104]; Sobre gustos no hay nada escrito [108]; No hay nada que no esté ya dicho [112].

NADIE: Nadie se alabe hasta que acabe [15].

NARIZ: Me tiene agarrado por las narices [39].

NATURALEZA: La costumbre es otra naturaleza [33].

NEGOCIO: El negocio es el negocio [13].

NINGUNA: Ninguna nueva, buenas nuevas [78].

NIÑO: Lo que el niño oyó en el hogar, eso dice en el portal [19].

NOCHE: La noche trae consejo [77].

NOVIA: Muchos componedores descomponen la novia [115].

NUEVA (adjetivo): Escoba nueva barre bien [76].

NUEVA (sustantivo): Ninguna nueva, buenas nuevas [78].

NUNCA: Más vale tarde que nunca [11]; Nunca es tarde para aprender [75].

OCASION: La ocasión hace al ladrón [89].

OCIOSIDAD: Muchos males engendra la ociosidad [14].

ODIOSA: Toda comparación es odiosa [21].

OIR: Lo que el niño oyó en el hogar, eso dice en el portal [19]; No hay peor sordo que el que no quiere oír [81]; Las paredes oyen [117].

OJO: Se llena antes el papo que el ojo [23]; Cuatro ojos ven más que dos [28]; Ojos que no ven, corazón que no siente [91].

OLVIDAR (se): El primer amor es el último en olvidarse [82].

OLLA: Cada ollero su olla alaba [22].

OLLERO: Cada ollero su olla alaba [22].

OREJA: Me ha echado la pulga detrás de la oreja [41].

ORO: La palabra es de plata, el silencio es de oro [105].

OSO: Me reparto la piel del oso antes de cazarlo [54].

OTORGAR: Quien calla, otorga [103].

OTRO: Un favor se paga con otro [85]; A otros tiempos, otras costumbres [90].

OVEJA: Cada oveja con su pareja [12]; En cada rebaño hay una oveja descarriada [110]; Un lobo con piel de oveja [127].

PACIENCIA: Con la paciencia todo se alcanza [93]; La paciencia tiene un límite [111].

PAGAR: Un favor se paga con otro [85].

PALABRA: La palabra es de plata, el silencio es de oro [105].

PALO: De tal palo, tal astilla [60]; En casa del herrero, cuchara de palo [102]; El asno y la mujer, a palos se han de vencer [128].

PAN: A falta de pan buenas son tortas [9]; A buen hambre no hay pan duro [51].

PAPO: Se llena antes el papo que el ojo [23].

PARED: Las paredes oyen [117].

PAREJA: Cada oveja con su pareja [12].

PAZ: Si quieres la paz, prepárate para la guerra [52].

PEDIR: Pide lo más y algo te darán [5].

PELAR: Mientras hace calor se pelan los árboles [66].

PELEAR: No es bueno pelear por un hueso [57].

PENSAMIENTO: Los segundos pensamientos son los mejores [100].

PEOR: No hay peor ciego que el que no quiere ver [80]; No hay peor sordo que el que no quiere oír [81].

PERDER: Desnudo nací, desnudo me hallo, ni pierdo ni gano [74].

PERRO: El perro puede mirar al rey [17]; Quien con perros se acuesta, con pulgas se levanta [44]; Perro ladrador, poco mordedor [126].

PIE: Está con un pie en la sepultura [38]; No hay que buscar tres pies al gato [58].

PIEL: Me reparto la piel del oso antes de cazarlo [54]; Un lobo con piel de oveja [127].

PLANTA: Viejas plantas traspuestas, ni crecen ni medran [98].

PLATA: La palabra es de plata, el silencio es de oro [105].

POCO: Perro ladrador, poco mordedor [126].

PODER: Quien compra lo que no puede, vende lo que le duele [43]; No dejes para mañana lo que puedes hacer hoy [73]; Querer es poder [124].

POLLO: Mejor es huevo hoy que pollo mañana [8].

PORTAL: Lo que el niño oyó en el hogar, eso dice en el portal [19].

PREPARAR (se): Si quieres la paz, prepárate para la guerra [52].

PREVENIR: Más vale prevenir que curar [96].

PRIMERO: El primer venido, primer servido [26]; Primero es la salud que el dinero [35]; El primer amor es el último en olvidarse [82].

PRISA: Vísteme despacio, que tengo prisa [71].

PROPIA: Se cuece en su propia salsa [36].

PUERTA: El dinero abre todas las puertas [70]; Cuando el hambre entra por la puerta, el amor huye por la ventana [122].

PULGA: Me ha echado la pulga detrás de la oreja [41]; Quien con perros se acuesta, con pulgas se levanta [44].

QUERER: Caballo que vuela, no quiere espuelas [31]; Si quieres la paz, prepárate para la guerra [52]; Quien quiere a Beltrán, quiere a su can [64]; No hay peor ciego que el que no quiere ver [80]; No hay peor sordo que el que no quiere oír [81]; Querer es poder [124].

RAIZ: La avaricia es la raíz de todos los males [69].

RATA: Las ratas abandonan el barco que se hunde [97].

RATON: Cuando el gato no está, los ratones bailan [123].

REBAÑO: En cada rebaño hay una oveja descarriada [110].

RECIBIR: Más bienaventurada cosa es dar que recibir [56].

REPARTIR (se):
Me reparto la piel del oso antes de cazarlo [54].

REPENTE (de): Al hierro caliente, batir de repente [106].

REY: El perro puede mirar al rey [17].

RICA: En casa de mujer rica, ella manda y ella grita [45].

RISA: Cosa hecha aprisa, cosa de risa [34].

ROMA: Cuando a Roma fueres, haz como vieres [121].

ROSA: No hay rosa sin espinas [79].

RUIN: El fuego y el agua son buenos servidores pero ruines amos [25].

SALARIO: A tal trabajo, tal salario [3].

SALSA: Se cuece en su propia salsa [36].

SALTAR: Mirar antes de saltar [63].

SALUD: Primero es la salud que el dinero [35].

SEGUNDO: Los segundos pensamientos son los mejores [100].

SENTIR: Ojos que no ven, corazón que no siente [91].

SEPARAR: El tonto y su dinero son pronto separados [27].

SEPULTURA: Está con un pie en la sepultura [38].

SERVIDO: El primer venido, primer servido [26].

SERVIDOR: El fuego y el agua son buenos servidores pero ruines amos [25].

SETO: Ama tu vecino pero no deshagas tu seto [65].

SIEMBRA: Hay quien siembra y quien cosecha [87].

SILENCIO: La palabra es de plata, el silencio es de oro [105].

SOLO: Mejor solo que mal acompañado [7].

SORDO: No hay peor sordo que el que no quiere oír [81].

SUCIO: Los trapos sucios se lavan en casa [86].

TAL... TAL: A tal trabajo, tal salario [3]; De tal palo, tal astilla [60]; A tal dama, tal criada [61].

TARDE: Más vale tarde que nunca [11]. Nunca es tarde para aprender [75].

TENER: Me tiene agarrado por las narices [39]; Vísteme despacio, que tengo prisa [71].

TIEMPO: A otros tiempos, otras costumbres [90]; Hay un tiempo para hablar y un tiempo para callar [113].

TOMAR: Consejo, tómalo de hombre viejo [53]; Tomemos las cosas como vienen [118].

TONTO: El tonto y su dinero son pronto separados [27].

TORNAR: La vejez tornó por los días en que nació [83].

TORTA: A falta de pan, buenas son tortas [9].

TORTILLA: No se hacen tortillas sin huevos [84].

TRABAJO: A tal trabajo, tal salario [3].

TRAER: La noche trae consejo [77].

TRAPO: Los trapos sucios se lavan en casa [86].

TRASPUESTA: Viejas plantas traspuestas, ni crecen ni medran [98].

ULTIMO: El primer amor es el último en olvidarse [82].

UNION: La unión hace la fuerza [116].

VARIEDAD: En la variedad está el gusto [32].

VECINO: Ama tu vecino pero no deshagas tu seto [65].

VEJEZ: La vejez tornó por los días en que nació [83].

VENCER: El asno y la mujer, a palos se han de vencer [128].

VENDER: Quien compra lo que no puede, vende lo que le duele [43].

VENIR: El primer venido, primer servido [26]. Tomemos las cosas como vienen [118].

VENTANA: Cuando el hambre entra por la puerta, el amor huye por la ventana [122].

VER: Cuatro ojos ven más que dos [28]; No hay peor ciego que el que no quiere ver [80]; Ojos que no ven, corazón que no siente [91]; Ver es creer [101]; Cuando a Roma fueres, haz como vieres [121].

VERANO: Una golondrina no hace verano [88].

VERDAD: En el vino está la verdad [55].

VESTIR (se): Vísteme despacio, que tengo prisa [71].

VIAJAR: Viajando se instruye la gente [48].

VIDA: El arte es largo y la vida breve [59].

VIEJO: Consejo, tómalo del hombre viejo [53]; Viejas plantas traspuestas, ni crecen ni medran [98].

VINO: En el vino está la verdad [55].

VIVIR: No hay que vivir para comer, sino comer para vivir [62].

VOLAR: Caballo que vuela, no quiere espuelas [31].

VULPEJA: A la vulpeja dormida no le cae nada en la boca [104].

YA: No hay nada que no esté ya dicho [112].

YACER: Quien mala cama hace, en ella yace [4].

ITALIANO

ABBANDONARE: I topi abbandonano la nave che affonda [97].

ABITO: L'abito fa l'uomo [29].

ABITUDINE: L'abitudine è una seconda natura [33].

ACCOMPAGNATO: Meglio soli che male accompagnati [7].

ACCONSENTIRE: Chi tace, acconsente [103].

ACCUSARE (-rsi): Chi si scusa, si accusa [46].

ACQUA: Il fuoco e l'acqua son buoni servitori, ma cattivi padroni [25].

AFFARE: Gli affari sono affari [13]; Non ficcare il naso negli affari altrui [107].

AFFONDARE: I topi abbandonano la nave che affonda [97].

AGIRE: Chi parla molto, agisce poco [126].

AGNELLO: Un lupo travestito da agnello [127].

ALBERO: Trapianta un albero vecchio, e lo vedrai morire [98].

ALLOGGIARE: Chi tardi arriva, male alloggia [26].

ALTRO: Altri tempi, altri costumi [90].

ALTRUI: Non ficcare il naso negli affari altrui [107].

AMARE: Chi ama me, ama il mio cane [64].

AMORE: Il primo amore non si scorda mai [82].

ANDARE (-rsene): Non son tutti santi quelli che vanno in chiesa [1]; Se n'è andato all'inglese [42]; Dimmi con chi vai, e ti dirò chi sei [109]; Quando la fame entra dalla porta, l'amore se ne va dalla finestra [122].

APPARECCHIARE: Chi vuol la pace, apparecchi la guerra [52].

APRIRE: Il denaro apre tutte le porte [70].

ARGENTO: La parola è d'argento, il silenzio è d'oro [105].

ARMATO: È armato fino ai denti [37].

ARRIVARE: Chi tardi arriva, male alloggia [26].

ARTE: La vita è breve, l'arte è lunga [59].

ASINO: Donne, asini e noci voglion le mani atroci [128].

ASSAI: Chi vuole assai, non domandi poco [5].

ATROCE: Donne, asini e noci voglion le mani atroci [128].

AVARIZIA: L'avarizia è la radice di tutti i mali [69].

AVERE: Non dire quattro se non l'hai nel sacco [72].

BALLARE: Quando non c'è il gatto, i topi ballano [123].

BAMBINO: I bambini ripetono ciò che hanno sentito in casa [19].

BATTERE: Bisogna battere il ferro finché è caldo [106].

BELLEZZA: La bellezza è effimera [6].

BENE: Tutto è bene quel che finisce bene [2]; Scopa nuova scopa bene [76]; Chi ben comincia, è a metà dell'opra [119]; Chi si sposa fa bene, chi non si sposa fa meglio [125].

BENVENUTO: Chi porta, è sempre il benvenuto [114].

BIANCO: Le preoccupazioni fanno venire i capelli bianchi [16].

BOCCA: Ha gli occhi più grandi della bocca [23].

BREVE: La vita è breve, l'arte è lunga [59].

BRODO: Bisogna lasciarlo cuocere nel suo brodo [36].

BUONO: Il fuoco e l'acqua son buoni servitori, ma cattivi padroni [25]; Nessuna nuova, buona nuova [78].

CALDO: Mani fredde, cuore caldo [20]; Bisogna battere il ferro finché è caldo [106].

CALZOLAIO: Il calzolaio ha le scarpe rotte [102].

CAMPAGNA: Dio fece la campagna, l'uomo fece la città [30].

CANE: Chi va a letto con i cani, si leva con le pulci [44]; Non svegliare il can che dorme [58]; Chi ama me, ama il mio cane [64].

CAPELLO: Le preoccupazioni fanno venire i capelli bianchi [16]; Ha debiti fin sopra i capelli [92].

CARITÀ: La prima carità comincia da se stessi [18].

CASA: I bambini ripetono ciò che hanno sentito in casa [19];

Dalla casa si conosce il padrone [50]; I panni sporchi si lavano in casa [86].

CATTIVO: Il fuoco e l'acqua son buoni servitori, ma cattivi padroni [25].

CAUSARE: La troppa fretta spesso causa ritardo [71].

CAVALLO: Caval che corre non ha bisogno di sprone [31].

CERCARE: Chi cerca, trova [47].

CHIAMARE: I soldi chiamano soldi [68].

CHIEDERE: Chiedi consiglio a chi è vecchio [53].

CHIESA: Non son tutti santi quelli che vanno in chiesa [1].

CIECO: Non c'è peggior cieco di chi non vuol vedere [80].

CITTÀ: Dio fece la campagna, l'uomo fece la città [30].

COMINCIARE: La prima carità comincia da se stessi [18]; Chi ben comincia, è a metà dell'opra [119].

COMPRARE: Chi compra il superfluo, venderà il necessario [43].

CONFIDENZA: Troppa confidenza toglie riverenza [24].

CONFRONTO: I confronti sono odiosi [21].

CONOSCERE: Dalla casa si conosce il padrone [50].

CONSIGLIO: Chiedi consiglio a chi è vecchio [53]; La notte porta consiglio [77]; Dopo il fatto, il consiglio non vale [120].

CORRERE: Caval che corre non ha bisogno di sprone [31].

COSTUME: Altri tempi, altri costumi [90].

CREDERE: Quel che l'occhio vede, il cuore crede [101].

CUOCERE: Bisogna lasciarlo cuocere nel suo brodo [36].

CUOCO: La fame è il miglior cuoco [51]; Troppi cuochi rovinano la minestra [115].

CUORE: Mani fredde, cuore caldo [20]; Lontano dagli occhi, lontano dal cuore [91]; Quel che l'occhio vede, il cuore crede [101].

CURARE: Medico, cura te stesso [94].

DARE: Si prova più gioia a dare che a ricevere [56]; Io dò una mano a te, tu dai una mano a me [99].

DEBITO: Ha debiti fin sopra i capelli [92].

DENARO: Il pazzo e il suo denaro son presto separati [27]; Il denaro apre tutte le porte [70].

DENTE: È armato fino ai denti [37].

DIO: Dio fece la campagna, l'uomo fece la città [30].

DIRE: Non dire quattro se non l'hai nel sacco [72]; Dimmi con chi vai, e ti dirò chi sei [109]; Non c'è niente che non sia già stato detto [112].

DIVENTARE: È con l'esercizio che si diventa maestri [95].

DOMANDARE: Chi vuole assai, non domandi poco [5].

DOMANI: Meglio un uovo oggi che una gallina domani [8]; Non rimandare a domani quel che potresti fare oggi [73].

DONNA: Donne, asini e noci voglion le mani atroci [128].

DORMIRE: Come uno si fa il letto, così dorme [4]; Non svegliare il can che dorme [58]; Chi dorme, non piglia pesci [104].

DOTE: Dove entra dote, esce libertà [45].

DUE: Quattro occhi vedono più di due [28].

EFFIMERO: La bellezza è effimera [6].

ENTRARE: Dove entra dote, esce libertà [45]; Quando la fame entra dalla porta, l'amore se ne va dalla finestra [122].

ESERCIZIO: È con l'esercizio che si diventa maestri [95].

FAME: La fame è il miglior cuoco [51]; Quando la fame entra dalla porta, l'amore se ne va dalla finestra [122].

FANCIULLO: I vecchi son due volte fanciulli [83].

FARE (-rsi): Come uno si fa il letto, così dorme [4]; Dio fece la campagna, l'uomo fece la città [30]; Non rimandare a domani quel che potresti fare oggi [73]; Non si fanno frittate senza rompere uova [84]; Una rondine non fa primavera [88]; L'occasione fa l'uomo ladro [89]; L'unione fa la forza [116]; Quando a Roma andrai, fa' come vedrai [121].

FATTO: Dopo il fatto, il consiglio non vale [120].

FAVORE: A un favore si risponde con un altro favore [85].

FELICE: Nessuno può dirsi felice a questo mondo [15].

FERRO: Bisogna battere il ferro finché è caldo [106].

FICCARE: Non ficcare il naso negli affari altrui [107].

FIENO: Bisogna tagliare il fieno finché non piove [66].

FIGLIA/FIGLIO: Tale il padre, tale il figlio; tale la madre, tale la figlia [60].

FINESTRA: Quando la fame entra dalla porta, l'amore se ne va dalla finestra [122].

FINIRE: Tutto è bene quel che finisce bene [2].

FORZA: L'unione fa la forza [116].

FOSSA: Ha un piede nella fossa [38].

FREDDO: Mani fredde, cuore caldo [20].

FRETTA: Troppa fretta nuoce [34]; La troppa fretta spesso causa ritardo [71].

FRITTATA: Non si fanno frittate senza rompere uova [84].

FUOCO: Il fuoco e l'acqua son buoni servitori, ma cattivi padroni [25].

GALLINA: Meglio un uovo oggi che una gallina domani [8].

GATTO: Anche un gatto può guardare un re [17].

GIÀ: Non c'è niente che non sia già stato detto [112].

GIOIA: Si prova più gioia a dare che a ricevere [56].

GRANDE: Ha gli occhi più grandi della bocca [23].

GREGGE: In ogni gregge c'è una pecora nera [110].

GUARDARE: Anche un gatto può guardare un re [17].

GUERRA: Chi vuol la pace, apparecchi la guerra [52].

GUSTO: Ognuno ha i suoi gusti [108].

IDEA: La seconda idea è sempre la migliore [100].

IMPARARE: Sbagliando s'impara [67]; Non si è mai troppo vecchi per imparare [75].

INGLESE: Se n'è andato all'inglese [42].

INIMICIZIA: Vicinanza senza siepe porta inimicizia in casa [65].

ISTRUIRE (-rsi): Chi viaggia, si istruisce [48].

LADRO: Cento ladri non possono spogliare un uomo nudo [74].

LAVARE: I panni sporchi si lavano in casa [86].

LAVORO: Tale il lavoro, tale il salario [3].

LETTO: Come uno si fa il letto, così dorme [4]; Chi va a letto con i cani, si leva con le pulci [44].

LEVARE (-rsi): Chi va a letto con i cani, si leva con le pulci [44].

LIBERTÀ: Dove entra dote, esce libertà [45].

LIMITE: Anche la pazienza ha un limite [111].

LITIGARE: Non val la pena di litigare per un osso [57].

LODARE: Ognuno loda il suo operato [22].

LONTANO: Lontano dagli occhi, lontano dal cuore [91].

LUNGO: La vita è breve, l'arte è lunga [59].

LUPO: Un lupo travestito da agnello [127].

MADRE: Tale il padre, tale il figlio; tale la madre, tale la figlia [60].

MAESTRO: È con l'esercizio che si diventa maestri [95].

MAI: Meglio tardi che mai [11]; Non si è mai troppo vecchi per imparare [75].

MALE (avv.): Meglio soli che male accompagnati [7]; Chi tardi arriva, male alloggia [26].

MALE (sost.): L'avarizia è la radice di tutti i mali [69].

MANGIARE: Si deve mangiare per vivere, non vivere per mangiare [62].

MANO: Mani fredde, cuore caldo [20]; Io dò una mano a te, tu dai una mano a me [99]; Donne, asini e noci voglion le mani atroci [128].

ME: Chi ama me, ama il mio cane [64]; Io dò una mano a te, tu dai una mano a me [99].

MEDICO: Medico, cura te stesso [94].

MENARE: Mi sta menando per il naso [39].

METÀ: Chi ben comincia, è a metà dell'opra [119].

METTERE: Mi ha messo una pulce nell'orecchio [41].

MIGLIORE: L'onestà è la miglior moneta [49]; La fame è
il miglior cuoco [51]; La seconda idea è sempre
la migliore [100].

MINESTRA: Troppi cuochi rovinano la minestra [115].

MOLTO: Chi parla molto, agisce poco [126].

MONDO: Nessuno può dirsi felice a questo mondo [15];
Bisogna prendere il mondo come viene [118].

MONETA: L'onestà è la miglior moneta [49].

MORIRE: Trapianta un albero vecchio, e lo vedrai morire [98].

MURO: I muri hanno orecchi [117].

NASO: Mi sta menando per il naso [39]; Non ficcare il naso
negli affari altrui [107].

NATURA: L'abitudine è una seconda natura [33].

NAVE: I topi abbandonano la nave che affonda [97].

NECESSARIO: Chi compra il superfluo, venderà
il necessario [43].

NERO: In ogni gregge c'è una pecora nera [110].

NESSUNO: Nessuno può dirsi felice a questo mondo [15];
Nessuna nuova, buona nuova [78].

NIENTE: Meglio poco che niente [9]; Non c'è niente che non
sia già stato detto [112].

NOCE: Donne, asini e noci voglion le mani atroci [128].

NOTTE: La notte porta consiglio [77].

NUOCERE: Troppa fretta nuoce [34].

NUOVA (nome): Nessuna nuova, buona nuova [78].

NUOVO (agg.): Scopa nuova scopa bene [76].

NUDO: Cento ladri non possono spogliare un uomo nudo [74].

OCCASIONE: L'occasione fa l'uomo ladro [89].

OCCHIO: Ha gli occhi più grandi della bocca [23];
Quattro occhi vedono più di due [28]; Lontano dagli occhi,
lontano dal cuore [91]; Quel che l'occhio vede,

il cuore crede [101].

ODIOSO: I confronti sono odiosi [21].

OGGI: Meglio un uovo oggi che una gallina domani [8];
Non rimandare a domani quel che potresti fare oggi [73].

OGNUNO: Ognuno loda il suo operato [22]; Ognuno ha
i suoi gusti [108].

ONESTÀ: L'onestà è la miglior moneta [49].

ONORATO: Meglio povertà onorata che ricchezza
svergognata [10].

OP(E)RA: Chi ben comincia, è a metà dell'opra [119].

OPERATO: Ognuno loda il suo operato [22].

ORECCHIO: Mi ha messo una pulce nell'orecchio [41];
I muri hanno orecchi [117].

ORO: La parola è d'argento, il silenzio è d'oro [105].

ORSO: Non vendere la pelle dell'orso prima d'averlo
preso [54].

OSSO: Non val la pena di litigare per un osso [57].

OTTENERE: Con la pazienza si ottiene tutto [93].

OZIO: L'ozio è il padre dei vizi [14].

PACE: Chi vuol la pace, apparecchi la guerra [52].

PADRE: L'ozio è il padre dei vizi [14]; Tale il padre, tale
il figlio; tale la madre, tale la figlia [60].

PADRONA: Tale la padrona, tale la serva [61].

PADRONE: Il fuoco e l'acqua son buoni servitori, ma cattivi
padroni [25]; Dalla casa si conosce il padrone [50].

PANNO: I panni sporchi si lavano in casa [86].

PARLARE: C'è un tempo per parlare e un tempo per
tacere [113]; Chi parla molto, agisce poco [126].

PAROLA: La parola è d'argento, il silenzio è d'oro [105].

PAZIENZA: Con la pazienza si ottiene tutto [93]; Anche la
pazienza ha un limite [111].

PAZZO: Il pazzo e il suo denaro son presto separati [27].

PECORA: In ogni gregge c'è una pecora nera [110].

PEGGIORE: Non c'è peggior cieco di chi non vuol vedere [80];
Non c'è peggior sordo di chi non vuol sentire [81].

PELLE: Non vendere la pelle dell'orso prima d'averlo preso [54].

PENSARE: Bisogna pensarci prima per non pentirsi poi [63].

PENTIRSI: Bisogna pensarci prima per non pentirsi poi [63].

PESCE: Chi dorme, non piglia pesci [104].

PIACERE: Il piacere sta nella varietà [32].

PIEDE: Ha un piede nella fossa [38].

PIGLIARE: Chi dorme, non piglia pesci [104].

PIOVERE: Bisogna tagliare il fieno finché non piove [66].

POCO: Chi vuole assai, non domandi poco [5]; Meglio poco che niente [9]; Chi parla molto, agisce poco [126].

PORTA: Il denaro apre tutte le porte [70]; Quando la fame entra dalla porta, l'amore se ne va dalla finestra [122].

PORTARE: La notte porta consiglio [77]; Chi porta, è sempre il benvenuto [114].

POTERE: Volere è potere [124].

POVERTÀ: Meglio povertà onorata che ricchezza svergognata [10].

PRENDERE: Non vendere la pelle dell'orso prima d'averlo preso [54]; Bisogna prendere il mondo come viene [118].

PREOCCUPAZIONE: Le preoccupazioni fanno venire i capelli bianchi [16].

PRESTO: Il pazzo e il suo denaro son presto separati [27].

PREVENIRE: Meglio prevenire che reprimere [96].

PRIMAVERA: Una rondine non fa primavera [88].

PRIMO: Il primo amore non si scorda mai [82].

PULCE: Mi ha messo una pulce nell'orecchio [41]; Chi va a letto con i cani, si leva con le pulci [44].

QUATTRO: Quattro occhi vedono più di due [28]; Non dire quattro se non l'hai nel sacco [72].

RACCOGLIERE: C'è chi semina e c'è chi raccoglie [87].

RADICE: L'avarizia è la radice di tutti i mali [69].

RE: Anche un gatto può guardare un re [17].

REPRIMERE: Meglio prevenire che reprimere [96].

RICCHEZZA: Meglio povertà onorata che ricchezza svergognata [10]; La salute val più della ricchezza [35].

RICEVERE: Si prova più gioia a dare che a ricevere [56].

RIMANDARE: Non rimandare a domani quel che potresti fare oggi [73].

RIPETERE: I bambini ripetono ciò che hanno sentito in casa [19].

RISPONDERE: A un favore si risponde con un altro favore [85].

RITARDO: La troppa fretta spesso causa ritardo [71].

RIVERENZA: Troppa confidenza toglie riverenza [24].

ROMA: Quando a Roma andrai, fa' come vedrai [121].

ROMPERE: Non si fanno frittate senza rompere uova [84].

RONDINE: Una rondine non fa primavera [88].

ROSA: Non c'è rosa senza spine [79].

ROTTO: Il calzolaio ha le scarpe rotte [102].

ROVINARE: Troppi cuochi rovinano la minestra [115].

SACCO: Non dire quattro se non l'hai nel sacco [72].

SALARIO: Tale il lavoro, tale il salario [3].

SALUTE: La salute val più della ricchezza [35].

SANTO: Non son tutti santi quelli che vanno in chiesa [1].

SBAGLIARE: Sbagliando s'impara [67].

SCARPA: Il calzolaio ha le scarpe rotte [102].

SCOPA/SCOPARE: Scopa nuova scopa bene [76].

SCORDARE: Il primo amore non si scorda mai [82].

SCUSARE (-rsi): Chi si scusa, si accusa [46].

SECONDO: L'abitudine è una seconda natura [33]; La seconda idea è sempre la migliore [100].

SEMINARE: C'è chi semina e c'è chi raccoglie [87].

SENTIRE: I bambini ripetono ciò che hanno sentito in casa [19]; Non c'è peggior sordo di chi non vuol sentire [81].

SEPARARE: Il pazzo e il suo denaro son presto separati [27].

SERVA: Tale la padrona, tale la serva [61].

SERVITORE: Il fuoco e l'acqua son buoni servitori, ma cattivi padroni [25].

SIEPE: Vicinanza senza siepe porta inimicizia in casa [65].

SILENZIO: La parola è d'argento, il silenzio è d'oro [105].

SIMILE: I simili vanno con i simili [12].

SOLDI: I soldi chiamano soldi [68].

SOLO: Meglio soli che male accompagnati [7].

SORDO: Non c'è peggior sordo di chi non vuol sentire [81].

SPINA: Sta sulle spine [40]; Non c'è rosa senza spine [79].

SPOGLIARE: Cento ladri non possono spogliare un uomo nudo [74].

SPORCO: I panni sporchi si lavano in casa [86].

SPOSARE (-rsi): Chi si sposa fa bene, chi non si sposa fa meglio [125].

SPRONE: Caval che corre non ha bisogno di sprone [31].

SUPERFLUO: Chi compra il superfluo, venderà il necessario [43].

SVEGLIARE: Non svegliare il can che dorme [58].

SVERGOGNATO: Meglio povertà onorata che ricchezza svergognata [10].

TACERE: Chi tace, acconsente [103]; C'è un tempo per parlare e un tempo per tacere [113].

TALE... TALE...: Tale il lavoro, tale il salario [3];
Tale il padre, tale il figlio; tale la madre, tale la figlia [60];
Tale la padrona, tale la serva [61].

TARDI: Meglio tardi che mai [11]; Chi tardi arriva, male alloggia [26].

TE: Io dò una mano a te, tu dai una mano a me [99].

TEMPO: Altri tempi, altri costumi [90]; C'è un tempo per parlare e un tempo per tacere [113].

TOGLIERE: Troppa confidenza toglie riverenza [24].

TOPO: I topi abbandonano la nave che affonda [97]; Quando non c'è il gatto, i topi ballano [123].

TRAPIANTARE: Trapianta un albero vecchio, e lo vedrai morire [98].

TRAVESTITO: Un lupo travestito da agnello [127].

TROVARE: Chi cerca, trova [47].

UNIONE: L'unione fa la forza [116].

UOMO: L'abito fa l'uomo [29]; Dio fece la campagna, l'uomo fece la città [30]; Cento ladri non possono spogliare un uomo nudo [74]; L'occasione fa l'uomo ladro [89].

UOVO: Meglio un uovo oggi che una gallina domani [8]; Non si fanno frittate senza rompere uova [84].

USCIRE: Dove entra dote, esce libertà [45].

VALERE: La salute val più della ricchezza [35].

VARIETÀ: Il piacere sta nella varietà [32].

VECCHIO: Chiedi consiglio a chi è vecchio [53]; Non si è mai troppo vecchi per imparare [75]; I vecchi son due volte fanciulli [83]; Trapianta un albero vecchio, e lo vedrai morire [98].

VEDERE: Quattro occhi vedono più di due [28]; Non c'è peggior cieco di chi non vuol vedere [80]; Quel che l'occhio vede, il cuore crede [101]; Quando a Roma andrai, fa' come vedrai [121].

VENDERE: Chi compra il superfluo, venderà il necessario [43]; Non vendere la pelle dell'orso prima d'averlo preso [54].

VENIRE: Bisogna prendere il mondo come viene [118].

VERITAS (lat.): 'In vino veritas' (lat.) [55].

VIAGGIARE: Chi viaggia, si istruisce [48].

VICINANZA: Vicinanza senza siepe porta inimicizia in casa [65].

VINO: 'In vino veritas' (lat.) [55].

VITA: La vita è breve, l'arte è lunga [59].

VIVERE: Si deve mangiare per vivere, non vivere per mangiare [62].

VIZIO: L'ozio è il padre dei vizi [14].

VOLERE: Chi vuole assai, non domandi poco [5]; Chi vuol la pace, apparecchi la guerra [52]; Non c'è peggior cieco di chi non vuol vedere [80]; Non c'è peggior sordo di chi non vuol sentire [81]; Volere è potere [124]; Donne, asini e noci voglion le mani atroci [128].

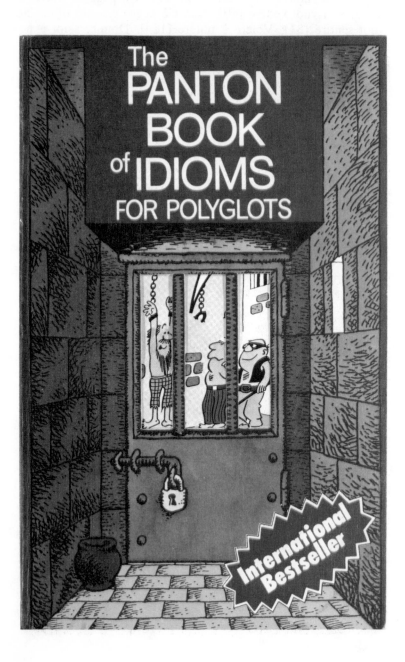

BOOK OF PUNGENT PROVERBS

Printed in Canada